HOLT ON:
THE PLANT PROTEIN REVOLUTION

Stephen Holt, MD

Published by the Holt Institute of Medicine, 2016

BOOK DATA

Copyright © Stephen Holt, MD, 2016, (in all languages)

Holt Institute of Medicine, www.hiom.org
25 Amity Street, Little Falls, New Jersey 07424
Tel.: 973-256-4660
Email: drholt@hiom.org

ISBN:0983079390

Printed in the United States of America

Published by the Holt Institute of Medicine, 2016 and Create Space Publishing Platform

KEY WORDS: 1. Plant Protein 2. Animal Protein 3. Chronic Disease 4. Wheat Protein 5. Hemp Protein 6. Rice Protein 7. Chia Protein 8. Pea Protein 9. Whey Protein 10. Soy Protein 11. Chlorella 12. Spirulina 13. Potato Protein 14. Quinoa 15. Gluten 16. Cardiovascular Disease 17. Cancer 18. Diabetes Mellitus 19. Osteoporosis 20. Functional Food 21. Allergies

PROLOGUE

THE ADOPTION OF PLANT PROTEIN INTAKE, AT THE EXPENSE OF ANIMAL PROTEIN, IN WESTERN DIETS, WILL HAVE A MAJOR POSITIVE IMPACT ON THE HEALTH OF MANY NATIONS.

STEPHEN HOLT 2015

CONTENTS

PROLOGUE

FOREWORD: • HENK HOOGENKAMP

PREFACE: • STEPHEN HOLT, MD

CHAPTER 1: • PROTEIN: GENERAL CONSIDERATIONS

CHAPTER 2: • SWITCHING TO PLANT PROTEIN DIETS

CHAPTER 3: • RICE PROTEIN

CHAPTER 4: • PEA PROTEIN

CHAPTER 5: • HEMP PROTEIN

CHAPTER 6: • SOY PROTEIN

CHAPTER 7: • WHEAT PROTEIN

CHAPTER 8: • OTHER PROTEINS

- EPILOGUE
- ABOUT THE AUTHOR
- OTHER BOOKS BY THE AUTHOR

FOREWORD

Henk Hoogenkamp, The Netherlands

For many years scientists have espoused many health advantages that ensue from the inclusion of plants, fruits and vegetables in the human diet. The trend has been to recommend a greater consumption of plant-based food in modern diets with a reduction of animal protein intake. This book focuses on the obvious benefits to be experienced with this modern change of food preference. In this book, Dr. Holt supports this dietary switch by a review of many human and animal experiments that illustrate the health benefits of a greater move towards plant-protein-based diets.

Among the foundations that support the recommendations of more plant proteins in the diet include healthy dietary components of fiber, micronutrients, minerals and phytochemicals, including antioxidants. Animal protein does not come with these diverse nutritional advantages to the same degree as plant protein, but it is associated with the health challenging components of excessive saturated fat and cholesterol. These dietary inclusions of fat and cholesterol together with other factors form a potential cardiovascular risk and other chronic diseases. In brief, this book presents a large body of evidence supports the occurrence of multiple health benefits with plant-protein-based diets which are preventive against a variety of cancers and free of carcinogens. Moreover, plant protein dietary inclusions appear to play a role in prevention of the modern epidemics of Type II diabetes mellitus and osteoporosis.

Existing diets in the U.S.A. and a number of other affluent societies often result in obesity, especially when combined with inactivity. As the nation's obesity pursues a relentless and destructive course, physicians and patients avidly seek a way out. For many years physicians and nutritionists have proposed plant protein diets for weight management or weight control, but until recently this approach has not been completely popularized. This book goes to a root source of the obesity problem by highlighting the role of many obesogenic Western diets with their unhealthy abundance of animal, egg and dairy protein. This modern Western diet is associated with the intake of high caloric loads.

While obesity "marches on" the importance of a diet for general health of the population is required in the U.S.A. In earlier work, Dr. Holt characterized the Soy Revolution (Holt, S., The Soy Revolution, Dell Publishing, Random House, Inc., 1998) and accurately predicted the growth of the use of soyfood and other plant protein sources as a pathway to enhanced well-being. This modern milestone in the application of plant-based food for health and disease prevention has now been expanded to further include the benefits of plant and vegetable protein in Dr. Holt's characterization of the emerging "Plant Protein Revolution."

The publication of this book is timely as epidemiologists in many countries grapple with National Survey Data, to examine the trends in the newfound quality of whole food, plant and protein intake in the diet. A dietary switch towards plant protein sources away from animal protein may go a long way towards changing the health of any nation.

>
> Henk Hoogenkamp
> The Netherlands
> Author of "Beyond Rice Protein", 2015 and
> "Plant Protein Vision", 2015

PREFACE

Stephen Holt, MD, New York, NY

Changing from animal to more plant protein inclusion in the human diet makes ecological and health sense. The Western diet has been criticized constantly concerning its over inclusion of calories, saturated fat, trans-fats, cholesterol, simple carbohydrates and animal protein. Scientists continue to enumerate the benefits of plant-based protein diets for the population at large, but only a limited number of people hear and act on this simple message. This circumstance creates a monumental task in any attempts to change the eating habits of a nation. While it is often difficult to pin-point the influence of certain or individual dietary constituents on health, it appears clear that strong carnivorous tendencies tend to breed ill health. The over inclusion of meat protein in the human diet presents excessive intake of saturated fat and cholesterol and it contributes to excess morbidity and mortality from cancer, diabetes mellitus, osteoporosis and cardiovascular disease.

While this book highlights the negative effects of excessive animal protein on health, it presents foundations to support the conclusion that a change towards plant protein intake will confer health benefits on the U.S. nation or much of Western society. The food industry has responded to the modern call for more plant protein intake with the development of protein sources from a variety of cereals, grains and legumes. This paradigm shift is only part of what I propose to be part of "The Plant Protein Revolution." Perhaps the ideal switch in sources of plant protein in the diet is to be achieved by utilizing whole food sources of protein, rather than extracted proteins. Extracted protein may sometimes be sourced from plants where proteins are nutritionally incomplete in terms of their contents of essential amino acids. Thus, there is much to be said for focusing on mixed, whole plant protein diets and avoid reductionist types of nutrition in the production of dietary staples.

To belabor the benefits of plant-based diets serves much purpose. High caloric loads, cholesterol and saturated fat contained in animal protein-based diets favor the development of chronic and often fatal diseases, such as cardiovascular events, type 2 diabetes mellitus, osteoporosis and cancer. These disorders cause much ill health and result from many factors including: high blood cholesterol, hypertension, insulin resistance (pre-diabetic state), oxidative stress, circumstances that favor carcinogenesis and other metabolic derangements (e.g. Metabolic Syndrome X). While many medical institutions and experts call for a collective support to improve diet in the U.S.A. only relatively small improvements have been achieved in the past decade or so (1999-2010). Moreover, while many experts speak about the health value of plant protein, a minority of people listens and even fewer make dietary changes.

There has been modest and recent improvement in dietary quality (1999-2010) in the U.S.A. This is most apparent in the more educated and affluent population (Dong Wang et al JAMA, Internal Medicine online publication, September 2014, hsph.harvard.edu/news/press release, Sept. 1, 2014). It is unfortunate that no increases in vegetable intake or decreases in red or processed meat intake were apparent in these recent Harvard studies (Dong Wang et al ibid 2014). Furthermore, an alarming finding in this research, was a recorded increase in salt intake. One major observation was the lack of effects of dietary improvements on the prevalence of obesity in the U.S.

Adjusting for the presence of adverse or positive lifestyle, it seems increasingly clear that research shows many health benefits of leaning towards a vegetarian diet. Vegetarian diets that are strict require careful planning to avoid specific nutrient deficiencies. In this respect, it is clear that the strict vegan may become deficient in vitamin B12 and limiting amino acids in some plant proteins need to be consumed to satisfy protein requirements for vital body functions. In spite of these and other potential shortcomings, a vegetarian diet is associated with several clear health benefits. Since the mainstay of vegetarian diets relate often to plant protein intake, with its associated nutrients and dietary fiber, compelling reasons continue to emerge to support the use of plant-based protein diets.

This book has a simple plot and it is split into eight chapters. The first two chapters review general aspects of dietary protein with an emphasis on the benefits of plant-based protein diet. Chapters three through eight review several of the main types of plant protein and their specific health properties. The conclusion of this book is clear. A dietary shift towards plant protein intake away from animal protein intake has many health promoting and disease prevention benefits. This desirable shift still remains a difficult task for most of Western society who remain somewhat brainwashed by tradition and the animal protein lobby. References in this book are used sometimes within the text, especially when they are directly relevant to specific statements. In addition, this book has reference sections by chapter that permits further examination of background information. This approach is designed to spare the reader the burden of many references quoted in the main text.

To dissect out the nutritional benefits of plant protein from whole forms of plant protein is a difficult task, given a degree of inadequate knowledge and factors other than diet that determine disease and mortality. The composition of plant protein is complemented in its actions by many other substances that are found in association with the protein itself. This book focuses on the many examples of this phenomenon in the face of the emerging "Plant Protein Revolution".

                                        Stephen Holt,
                                        Little Falls, New Jersey, August 2015

CHAPTER 1
PROTEIN: GENERAL CONSIDERATIONS

INTRODUCTION

Common proteins are macronutrients that provide essential and non-essential amino acids and they act as the principal dietary source of nitrogen. Proteins are macromolecules that are formed by the polymerization of amino acids in various combinations. Proteins have many different key and vital biological functions. Moreover, protein intake in the human diet is mandatory to supply amino acids that are necessary for the maintenance of general health, cellular integrity, and reproductive function.

Various sources of protein differ in their amino acid contents and, as a general rule, proteins of animal origin are "complete" in their content of essential amino acids, whereas plant proteins are often variably deficient in certain amino acids that cannot be synthesized by humans (essential amino acids). The growth of the world population makes plant and vegetable proteins of great ecological importance because plant proteins are a more abundant, ecofriendly and represent a more efficient source of amino acids than animal proteins. In other words, plant proteins are produced with a smaller ecological footprint than animal proteins.

There is no doubt that animal protein is a valuable "complete protein" for nutrition, but it has a reputation for being unhealthy because of its association in the diet with cholesterol, saturated fat and sometimes carcinogens (from cooking or processing). Several plant proteins are beginning to be favored by food scientists because these proteins are known to have high nutritional (biological) value and their associated properties are often health-giving in diverse ways - vide-infra. When plant proteins are combined in the diet they contain often sufficient quantities of essential amino acids for optimum nutrition. Thus, plant proteins are complementary and this circumstance highlights the importance of the intake of mixed plant protein diets.

The modern switch from animal to vegetable protein in the human diet has been occurring slowly in the food industry to a variable degree over the past three decades. This switch has occurred as a consequence of the widespread use of soy products and other types of plant protein. Moreover, soy (soya) has been demonstrated to have nutritional and health qualities equivalent to and often superior to animal protein (Holt, S., The Soy Revolution, Dell Publishing, Random House, 1999).

Some plant proteins have been overlooked as an efficient source of macronutrients because of their naturally occurring contents of anti-nutritive compounds. These compounds can act to limit the bioavailability (availability for the body) of soy components and other plant protein constituents. This situation decreases their nutritional value. However, modern food processing, selective plant breeding and genetic modifications have led to the greater elimination of anti-nutritive compounds in several types of plant or vegetable proteins. This has resulted in the greater availability of plant proteins with higher degrees of digestibility and improved bioavailability to meet requirements for human nutrition. However, genetic modification of plants and its potential consequences have become controversial and emotive issues for many people.

EMERGENCE OF PLANT PROTEIN PRODUCTS

Industrial processing methods of plant proteins such as soy, pea and rice have become increasingly sophisticated and they include low temperature extraction and enzymatic hydrolysis of insoluble proteins, after the removal of soluble protein. These processes allow the production of high concentration protein isolates and hydrolysates. The resulting protein products can be readily incorporated into a wide variety of foods, supplements, and medicinal products. With such processing, valuable nutrients contained in the whole plants may not be present in the extracted end products. This is an example of reductionist nutrition. A more profound example of reductionist nutrition often involves the use of dietary supplements.

In order to apply new plant protein products into sources of food or supplements, it is necessary to assess the absorption characteristics of the protein, particularly the bioavailability of the component amino acids. In addition, the toxicological profile of the plant protein must be studied and defined as safe. Access to this information can be used in the development of foods with special functions (functional food) for applications in sports nutrition and special nutritional circumstances. These special clinical or nutritional circumstances include the prevention of muscle loss (sarcopenia), especially in the elderly and the development of muscle gain (body building), with the combined use of protein and aerobic exercise.

Plant proteins contain many bioactive compounds which have a plethora of health benefits. These compounds include various antioxidants and healthy phytochemicals with specific beneficial activity. Such benefits include favorable additive effects on cardiovascular health by variable lowering blood lipids, lowering blood pressure, prevention of hypertension and benefits for weight control. In addition, vegetable or plant proteins may be helpful in the management of special metabolic disturbances, such as diabetes mellitus and the variable components of the metabolic syndrome (Syndrome X). Syndrome X or the metabolic syndrome is defined as the variable combination of an overweight status, hypertension and abnormal blood cholesterol profiles. In this circumstance of Metabolic Syndrome (Syndrome X), these disorders are linked in their presence by the occurrence of insulin resistance.

PROTEINS 101

Macronutrients in the diet are composed of carbon, hydrogen, and oxygen, but proteins are a principal source of nitrogen (about 16% total N). The composition of proteins results in the formation of many different compounds, which also contain micronutrients such as iron, phosphorous, sulfur, and cobalt. The nitrogen cycle of life involves the origin of dietary protein from primitive organisms, plants or animals. This protein undergoes metabolism and excretion by humans and many living organisms. This cycle returns nitrogen to the ecology.

PROTEIN STRUCTURE

Protein is composed mainly of alpha-amino carboxylic acids (except proline) and twenty, or so, such amino acids form most proteins. Amino acid chains are formed by peptide bonding where nitrogen and carboxylic acids are joined. The presence of this bonding leaves free carboxyl and amino groups which are capable of additions and deletions. Folding of amino acid chains produces secondary and tertiary structures of proteins. Many combinations of amino acids can occur in protein to produce molecules with different biological functions.

Hydrolysis of simple proteins results in free amino acids and polypeptide chains of varying length and composition (proteoses, polypeptides and peptones). Simple classes of proteins include varieties of albumin, globulin, glutelin, prolamin, and albuminoids. Proteins can be conjugated with prosthetic groups that provide specific functions of certain proteins. Examples of conjugated proteins include: nucleoproteins (RNA and DNA), mycoproteins, glycoproteins, lipoproteins, phosphoproteins, and metalloproteins (e.g. ferritin and hemosiderin).

While it is clear that proteins play an essential role in the structure of body tissues, and they also form enzymes, hormones, antibodies, and bioactive components of body fluids. A number of minerals and vitamins are attached to protein carriers, which transport these compounds or elements throughout the body. Specific roles of protein secretions include the maintenance of body homeostasis. This involves osmotic control of body fluids and acid-base balance.

TWO MAIN TYPES OF PROTEIN

Dietary protein is generally classified into two types, namely complete and incomplete sources of essential amino acids. Complete proteins contain all nine essential amino acids and are often referred to as "high quality" or premium proteins. These protein sources include protein sources such as meat, fish, eggs, poultry and concentrated dairy products, such as cheese. Incomplete proteins are absent or low in one or more of the essential amino acids. A class of proteins called complementary proteins involve two or more sources of protein, that when taken together, provide adequate amounts of all essential amino acids in the diet, e.g. rice and beans together.

Soy protein, for example, is a plant protein that is a complete protein, but other proteins of plant origin, such as rice protein, are lower in certain essential amino acids. As an example of "additive nutrition," it is recognized that beans can combine with rice as complementary protein sources in the diet and, to reiterate, this combination of plant proteins has a balanced protein content of all essential amino acids. It was once thought that complementary proteins could only fulfill their function as a complete protein when eaten together. However, many studies indicate that complementary proteins can be considered complete sources of amino acids when eaten on the same day or in reasonably close proximity to each other. Proteins are abundant in many foods. It is recommended that 10-35% of daily calorie intake comes from protein, but recommended daily allowances (RDA) of protein vary by age.

Age in Years	Grams/kg body weight	Grams/pound body weight
0.0-0.5	1.52	.69
0.5-1.0	1.10	.50
1-3	1.10	.50
4-8	0.95	.43
9-13	0.95	.43
14-18	0.85	.39
19 and up	0.8	.36

Table 1: Grams of protein needed per kilogram or pound body weight during the life cycle.

RECOMMENDED DAILY ALLOWANCE OF PROTEIN

There are many different opinions on the daily needs of protein intake. Recommended daily allowances (RDA) of protein may vary depending on variables such as age, pregnancy, growth needs, gender, presence of co-existing disease, etc. The RDA of protein has emerged from nitrogen balance studies that define needs of young male adults for certain reference proteins. Daily recommended intake of proteins has drifted upwards in the past 30 years. An average need for digestible, high quality protein as found in eggs, meat, milk products, or fish was defined in mid-1980s at about 0.61 g/kg of body weight per day. When amounts are adjusted for body weight, the needs of women were found to be similar to those of men.

A more recent recommendation for protein intake is 0.75 g/kg of total protein intake daily. This daily amount of protein is derived from the application of two standard deviations from mean (average) intakes, in order to meet the needs of 97.5% of the population. That said, **the acceptable general guideline for the RDA of protein in adults is about 0.8 grams per kilogram of body weight per day.** While residual arguments exist about the RDA of protein, one generally accepted recommendation is to ingest protein in amounts no more than twice the RDA, primarily to avoid the circumstances of "renal stress" and the development, in the long term, of osteoporosis. Renal "stress" due to excessive protein intake may be a factor (arguably) in the development of renal glomerulosclerosis. It is animal protein that is most likely to cause these problems when taken in excess.

As discussed earlier, the need for dietary protein differs at various stages in the human life cycle (Table 1). During infancy and adolescence, ample protein intake is required for growth. The need for protein intake stabilizes in early adulthood. During the life cycle leading to an adult status, the RDA of protein per unit of body weight decreases, but the total amount of protein requirements often increase as a consequence of increases in body weight. Table 1 summarizes the amount of protein required per kilogram of body weight at different ages. In recent years, interest has focused on the development of sarcopenia (and musculoskeletal problems) in the elderly. It has been suggested that the elderly (greater than 65 years of age) may receive some muscle-sparing benefit from increased protein intake to a level of 1-1.3 grams per day, especially later in life.

It is clear that individual protein needs vary and the efficiency of the overall utilization of protein tends to decrease at higher levels of dietary protein intake. There are guidelines on Acceptable Macronutrient Distribution Ranges (AMDR). These guidelines have been derived from epidemiological studies and nutrition intervention research. The AMDR are at levels that will prevent the occurrence of chronic disease by assuring the appropriate intake of essential nutrients. Furthermore, it has been mentioned earlier that protein needs are determined to a degree by total food energy intake. This defines an absolute need for adequate quality protein intake in individuals where energy intake is reduced.

THE ESSENTIAL AMINO ACIDS

Table 2 shows the 20 common amino acids that make up proteins. Essential amino acids cannot be made by the body and must be present in the diet. In some circumstances non-essential amino acids can become conditionally essential e.g. in newborns or in-born errors of amino acid metabolism e.g. phenylketonuria.

ESSENTIAL AMINO ACIDS	**NON ESSENTIAL AMINO ACIDS**
Histidine	Alanine
Isoleucine	Arginine
Leucine	Asparagine
Lysine	Aspartic acid
Methionine	Cysteine
Phenylalanine	Glutamic acid
Threonine	Glutamine
Tryptophan	Glycine

Valine   Serine

                                    Tyrosine

Table 2. Essential and non essential amino acids. Some amino acids may be conditionally essential e.g. in newborns.

Table 3 represents the RDA for the nine essential amino acids in a 70 kg adult male, but higher amounts are advisable for children and adolescents.

	RDA (mg/kg)	Total mg
Histidine	14	980
Isoleucine	19	1,260
Leucine	42	2,940
Lysine	38	2,660
Methionine (plus cysteine)	19	1,260
Phenylalanine (plus tyrosine)	33	2,310
Threonine	20	1,400
Tryptophan	5	350
Valine	24	1,680

Table 3: RDA for the essential amino acids in an adult male (70 kg)

It is suggested that about one quarter of the total daily protein requirement is most desirable in the form of essential amino acids (a conservative estimate is about 15g for an adult).

FUNCTIONS OF PROTEINS

Dietary protein supplies several functions which are summarized in Table 4. Principal functions of amino acids are the repair and building of tissue structures, manufacture of functional components that are involved in body chemistry (enzymes and hormones), and proteins are an important secondary source of energy.

Body Structure	Immune Function
Transport functions	Acid-Base balance
Enzymes	Fluid balance
Hormones	Energy source
Neurotransmitters	Muscle Function

Table 4: Main Functions of Proteins.

REDEFINING THE ROLE OF COMMON AMINO ACIDS

Certain amino acids are indispensable and come with obligatory nutritional needs. Absence of these indispensable (or essential amino acids) results in negative nitrogen balance, impaired growth, weight loss, and a variety of clinical symptoms and signs. Humans are unable to synthesize essential amino acids and nine different amino acids are defined as essential (Table 2). Essential amino acids include leucine, isoleucine, valine, tryptophan, phenylalanine, methionine, threonine, lysine, and histidine (Table 2). The amount of protein required to satisfy protein requirements is termed the Recommended Daily Allowance (RDA). It is clear that RDA varies depending on age, sex, coexisting medical disorders, levels of physical activity and alterations of body physiology.

There is a significant group of dispensable or non-essential amino acids which are an important part of normal protein structure (Table 5). Such amino acids can be synthesized variably by the human body, unlike essential amino acids. In addition, there are a group of amino acids that are considered to be conditionally dispensable that may prove to be indispensable under certain circumstances. As mentioned earlier, these circumstances include: infant growth, sepsis, recovery from trauma or surgery, or in the presence of malnutrition.

INDISPENSIBLE	CONDITIONALLY INDISPENSIBLE	DISPENSIBLE
Leucine	Proline	Glutamate
Isoleucine	Serine	Alanine
Valine	Arginine	Asparate
Tryptophan	Tyrosine	Glutamine
Phenylalanine	Cysteine	
Methionine	Taurine	
Threonine	Glycine	
Lysine		
Histidine		

Table 5: Classification of amino acids as essential (indispensable) and nonessential (conditionally indispensable and dispensable).

TYPES, ORIGIN AND SOURCES OF PROTEIN

Proteins are composed of chains of standard amino acids which tend to share a common structural feature. This feature involves the occurrence of an alpha carbon that is bonded with an amino group, a carboxyl group and a side chain of variable composition. These side chains are quite versatile and they are the principal determinant of the multidimensional structure, reactivity and function of the protein.

The pivotal factor in the nutritional value of proteins relates to its content or deficiency of essential amino acids (Table 5). Many forms of primitive life have an ability to synthesize twenty standard amino acids but, as mentioned earlier, many animals have an obligatory need of certain amino acids in their diet (essential amino acids). There are a number of enzymes that are present in micro-organisms that permit the synthesis of essential amino acids. For example, the enzyme aspartokinase is the catalyst for the synthesis of lysine, methionine and threonine from aspartic acid. Aspartokinase is not present in humans.

Protein structures are commonly defined as belonging to one of four different types, namely primarily, secondary, tertiary and quaternary. Structures of proteins determine their ultimate function. For example, the secondary structure of an alpha helix (right handed coiling) is found in keratins. These are examples of structural proteins present in hair and nails.

The most complex types of protein are quaternary forms which develop as a consequence of the interaction of adjacent molecules within the protein. A classic example of a complex structure is the substance hemoglobin. In a quaternary structure molecules are held together by hydrogen bonding, ionic bonding and Van der Waals Forces, with hydrophobic bonding holding together four subunits of this hemoglobin, macromolecular structure. This quaternary protein structure undergoes changes depending on oxygenation of hemoglobin. Overall, most proteins can be classified generally as structural or biological in their functions. In the preceding examples of protein structure, hemoglobin serves a biological and metabolic function, whereas keratin is a structural protein.

As mentioned earlier, the major distinguishing factor between animal and plant proteins is the presence of all essential amino acids in animal protein. In contrast, most plant proteins are deficient or low in one or more essential amino acids (limiting amino acids). Limiting amino acids are essential amino acids that are sometimes found in smaller amounts than those required for effective protein synthesis. The four amino acids that are most likely to be limiting are lysine, methionine, threonine and tryptophan. The variable lack in certain essential amino acids in plant proteins is often overcome by eating a mixture of plant proteins which have complementary benefits. This process of complementarity of proteins is very important in healthy diet planning.

About 10-35% of daily caloric intake should occur from protein sources. Table 6 lists the protein content of some common foods. There are groups of individuals with specific protein or nutritional needs, e.g. pregnant women, children during growth spurts, women breastfeeding, endurance athletes, body builders, individuals with specific metabolic needs as a consequence of trauma, sepsis or other illness. It is proposed that pregnant women should eat at least 10 grams extra of protein per day to support fetal development and an extra 20 grams per day during breastfeeding. Table 6 shows the protein content of common foods

FOOD	PROTEIN (GRAMS)
Milk, 244g (8 oz.)	8.0
Cheddar Cheese, 84g (3 oz.)	21.3
Egg, 50g (1 large)	6.1
Apple, 212g	0.4
Banana, 74g	1.2
Potato, cooked, 136g (1 potato)	2.5
Bread, white, slice, 25g	2.1
Fish, cod, poached, 100g (3 ½ oz.)	20.9
Oyster, 100g (3 ½ oz.)	13.5
Beef, pot roast, 85g (3 oz.)	22.0
Liver, pan fried, 85g (3 oz.)	23.0
Pork chop, bone in, 87g (3.1 oz.)	23.9
Ham, boiled, 2 pieces, 114g	20.0
Peanut butter, 16g (1 tablespoon)	4.6
Pecans, 28g (1 oz.)	2.2
Snap beans, 125g (1 cup)	2.4
Carrots, slicked, 78g (1/2 cup)	0.8

Source: U.S. Department of Agriculture

Table 6 Protein content of certain foods.

Attempts to counter muscle breakdown during heavy exercise have resulted in variable recommendations for extra protein intake. One rule of thumb is that endurance fitness enthusiasts consume an extra protein intake of 50% per day and bodybuilders an extra 100% per day, in comparison to a sedentary individual. Average or "normal" amounts of protein intake are 56 grams daily for a male adult and 46 grams per day for a female.

The CDC has suggested that two or three servings of protein rich food should be taken in the daily, average adult diet (Table 6). In brief, an eight ounce portion of steak or yogurt contains about 20 and 11 grams of protein, respectively. Furthermore, the body does not store protein in contrast to fats and carbohydrates.

There is continuing dialogue and difference of opinion about the advisability of high protein diets especially when consumed with the ketosis-provoking effects of carbohydrate restriction. Conservative opinion clings to the notion that extra protein intake is unhealthy and does not result in extra muscle strength in bodybuilders. It is proposed by many authorities that extra strength achieved by athletes is derived mainly from exercise.

In summary, animal sources of high quality, complete proteins (all essential amino acids) are found in meat, poultry, fish, eggs and milk. Plant sources of protein are very diverse in origin but are available to a significant degree in soy, different beans, whole grains, pulses, legumes, nuts, seed and fruits. As highlighted earlier, mixed plant diets may serve all essential amino acid needs when mixed in correct proportions in the diet (the concept of complementary proteins).

FOCUS ON PLANT PROTEIN SOURCES

It is estimated that 60% of total protein intake worldwide may come from plants. In contrast, in Western Europe and North America about 70-80% of total protein intake may come from animal sources. While protein of animal origin is complete protein, whole grains and cereals tend to be limited in their content of lysine or threonine (limiting amino acids). These limiting amino acids may also include tryptophan and sulfur containing amino acids. Cereal and staple protein sources are present in wheat, rice, buckwheat, oats, rye, millet, maize, bulgar sorghum, amaranth, quinoa, spaghetti and pasta. Other plant sources of protein include legumes, nuts and seeds (e.g. hemp or pumpkin seeds).

Overall, legumes have a higher content of mixed amino acids than grains, cereals or other staple foods. These vegetarian sources of protein include soy (complete protein), lentils, lupines, red and white beans, peas (pigeon and cow peas), lima beans, chickpeas, almonds, Brazil nuts, pecans, cashews, peanuts, pumpkin, sesame and sunflower seeds (Young, V., Pellett, P., Plant proteins in relation to human protein and amino acid nutrition, Am J. Clin. Nutr. 59, 1203-12, 1994).

In summary, it is generally agreed that efficient sources of protein are complete to provide a sustained supply of all essential amino acids and conditionally indispensable amino acids under "stressed circumstances" (physical or pathological). In addition, dietary protein has to supply nitrogen for the synthesis of dispensable amino acids and other essential compounds, e.g. creatine, porphyrins and nucleic acids (Young, V., Pellett, P., ibid, 1994).

To reiterate, one can stratify the important protein sources in certain food groups by the analysis of their limiting amino acid content. As discussed earlier, the commonest limiting amino acids include lysine, threonine, tryptophan and some sulfur containing amino acids. Measurement of the limiting amino acid per gram of total protein in the food source is a useful guide to the nutritive performance of proteins of various origin. For example, the lysine content of legumes is 64 mg per gram, with values of whole grains of 31, nuts of 45, fruit of 45 and animal protein of 85 (approximately).

ANIMAL PROTEIN ASSOCIATES WITH DIETARY FAT AND CHOLESTEROL

It is notable that animal protein intake comes along with excessive saturated fat and cholesterol intake, with often a high sodium (salt) load in the diet. The Centers for Disease Control and Prevention and other expert bodies recommend that individuals should be conscious of excessive fat intake along with animal protein. Among their suggestions to control fat intake with protein in the diet are: 1) to choose leaner cuts of meats, 2) to substitute beans for meat in certain dishes, e.g. tacos and chili con carne, 3) to select low fat or fat free milk and yogurt, 4) to moderate cheese intake and use low fat or fat free products, and 5) to select egg white protein over whole eggs. A useful source of guidelines is the Institute of Medicine Dietary Reference Intakes for Energy, Carbohydrate, Fiber, Fatty Acids, Fats, Cholesterol, Protein and Amino Acids (www.nap.edu).

Recent research continues to question the low fat or "fat free" diet for health. In fact, in 2015, American Dietary Guidelines were modified somewhat away from low fat and low cholesterol diets. In recent research, it has been found that the saturated fat (C-17 heptadecanoic acid) may be playing a role in reversal of Metabolic Syndrome X and resolution of diabetes-like states in dolphins. These findings have been extrapolated to humans (Venn-Watson S K et al, Increased Dietary Intake of Saturated Fatty Acid Heptadecanoic Acid (C17:0) Associated with Decreasing Ferrit in an Alleviated Metabolic Syndrome in Dolphins. PLOS ONE, 2015: 10(7): eoi 32117 DOI: 10.1371/journal pone 0132117). The saturated fat heptadecanoic acid is found in whole fat dairy products. There are an increasing number of advocates for balanced diets containing saturated fat and cholesterol.

PROBLEMS WITH WHEY PROTEIN SUPPLEMENTS

The common use of whey (milk) protein for muscle gain and weight loss possesses several disadvantages and limitations. Excessive whey protein intake is associated in some individuals with the development of unwanted weight gain or frank obesity. The calorie density of whey protein is high and this calorie intake often exceeds requirements for muscle building. The taste and ease of consumption of whey can easily lead to excessive consumption and weight gain.

While the high biological value rating (BV) of whey protein as a nutritional source of proteins in touted as advantageous (BV104, but up to 150), concerns have been expressed that excessive intake of whey protein can impair liver and renal function. It is generally accepted, in otherwise healthy athletes, that up to 2.8g per kg of body weight of whey will not impair renal function (Poortmans JR and Dellalieux O, Int J. Sport Nutr, March 2000). If compromised liver or renal function is present, the intake of protein should be revised downwards to recommend daily intakes or lower amounts. This circumstance may favor the use of protein with a lower biological value ratings (BV) such as rice protein (BV59). In brief, the Protein – Energy Ratio (PER) and biological value (BV) ratings are measures of how well proteins are absorbed and utilized by the body. With the use of PER and BV ratings "more" is not necessarily desirable.

One of the biggest and most common drawbacks to the use of whey protein involves its content of lactose. Lactose intolerance is quite common in the population, especially among Eastern Asians, and it is often hidden (occult) in foods. Lactose is digested by the enzyme lactase which is absent in individuals with lactose intolerance. In such individuals unabsorbed lactose can create havoc in the digestive tract where it is fermented to form short chain fatty acids. This failure to absorb lactose results in abdominal pain or cramps, excessive flatus (gas), bloating and diarrhea. This circumstance can be avoided by the use of soy, egg or other protein supplement use.

Whey protein is a milk derivative and in some individuals milk protein allergy is present. Milk, soy, and egg protein have a propensity to cause allergy, also, but rice protein is hypoallergenic in comparison with these other supplements. Symptoms and signs of milk protein allergy may be immediate with sneezing, throat irritation, coughing, eye itching and a running nose. Delayed signs of milk allergy include skin rashes and facial swelling. In rare circumstances anaphylactic shock can occur with life-threatening circulatory collapse.

There has been a suggestion that whey protein, unlike soy, rice and egg protein can lead to thin and weak bones (osteoporosis). This is believed to be due, in part, to the high content of sulphur-containing amino acids in whey which contribute to calcium loss. Increased protein consumption with whey can lead to hyperuricemia (high uric acid blood levels) and higher levels of amino acids in the body. Excessive blood acidity with high uric acid contributes to calcium release from bones which is a normal mechanism of keeping acid/base balance in check. Calcium loss from bones will promote the presence of osteoporosis, a highly undesirable, but putative effect, of whey protein excess.

Whey protein is known to cause drug interactions. It is documented that whey protein consumption can alter the absorption of certain antibiotics (tetracycline and norfloxacin) and interfere with the actions of levodopa (L Dopa). In some circumstances, whey consumption has been associated with hypoglycemia, increased bleeding risk in people with certain bleeding disorders and hypotension.

The Protein Digestibility Corrected Amino Acid Score (PDCAAS) and the Biological Value Ratings (BV) of proteins are benchmark measures of their nutritional properties. Whey protein has the highest PDCAAS and BV among all proteins. Other sources of protein, have variable, but lower, BV ratings of protein e.g. eggs (100), peanuts (68), wheat (54), soy protein (74), and rice protein (59).

PROBLEMS WITH EGG PROTEIN SUPPLEMENTS

Egg protein derived from the white portion of eggs contains approximately 4 gm of protein (egg size dependent) with a total calorie content of 16 Kcal. Unfortunately, egg allergies of variable severity are quite common. This prevalence of allergic reactions is slightly less than the occurrence of peanut or milk allergies. Allergy to eggs is most often accompanies by rash and hives (itchy skin bumps), but occasional cases of severe digestive upset are noted, with the rare occurrence of anaphylactic shock. The ingestion of large amounts of egg whites tends to cause constipation, gas and abdominal bloating and this makes egg protein an unacceptable single source of protein in several circumstances.

SPECIFIC AMINO ACID FUNCTIONS

Table 7 lists several amino acids with their specific functions:

AMINO ACID	FUNCTION
METHIONINE	A donor of methyl groups for the synthesis of creatinine or choline. A precursor of cysteine and other sulfur containing amino acids.
TRYPTOPHAN	A complex amino acid and precursor of niacin and serotonin.
PHENYLALANINE	A precursor of tyrosine, which is involved in the synthesis of epinephrine and thyroid hormones.
GLYCINE	Involved in porphyrin synthesis (hemoglobin) and detoxification.
HISTIDINE	A precursor of histamine.
CREATININE	Formed from methadone, arginine, and glycine and combines with phosphate to produce high energy phosphate in the cell (creatinine phosphate).
GLUTAMINE	A precursor of gamma-amino butyric acid (GABA) synthesized from glutamic acid and asparagines and involved in reservoir creation of amino acids.

Table 7: A partial list of specific functions of amino acids and related compounds.

PROTEIN INTAKE MUST BE ADEQUATE

In the best selling book "In Defense of Food", Michael Pollan highlights the multiple health benefits that occur by dietary switching to plant-based sources of nutrients. Pollan uses a powerful collective statement: **Eat food. Not too much. Mostly plants.** These words receive much clarification in Pollan's advice on what he terms "an eater's manifesto." Along with other authors (Lappe FM, Diet for a Small Planet, 1971 and 1982), Pollan plots an escape from Western Diets, but criticizes the concept of "nutritionism" as reductionist ideology. Nutritionism may ignore the value of whole foods, by the substitution of a language and concepts pertaining to key nutrients in food. That said, it is very difficult to enter any discussions of desirability of diet composition without some analysis of its principal contents that exert unique or individual effects on health and well-being.

It is clear that plant proteins have generally a lower content of essential amino acids compared with animal protein. Any deficiency of limiting amino acids such as methionine, lysine and tryptophan that can be encountered in plant proteins can result in reduced protein synthesis in humans. While lowering of scrum proteins is a theoretical risk of a reduced dietary intake of lysine and methionine, this circumstance has a preventive benefit against cardiovascular disease. This preventive benefit is related to cholesterol regulation due to inhibition of hepatic phospholipid metabolism. Control of blood homocysteine with plant-based diets also contributes to cardiovascular health.

Vegetarians tend to have a higher intake of non-essential amino acids such as arginine and pyruvate forming amino acids (notably, glycine, alanine and serine). The presence of high amounts of non-essential amino acids in plant protein will tend to down regulate the actions of insulin and upregulate those of glucagon. Stimulation of adenyl cyclase in these circumstances raises concentration of cyclic-AMP (adenosine monophosphate). This situation transmits overall in a reduction of other arteriosclerosis risk factors, such as cholesterol synthesis with upregulation of LDL receptors and decreases in IGF-1 (growth factor) activity. This latter effect on IGF-1 results in decreased cancer occurrence. Recent research has suggested that decreases in IGF-1 are protective against cancer, if such decreases are focused upon at the age range of 55-65 years, approximately.

Table 8 shows the protein content of selected vegan foods and also the number of grams of protein per 100 calories. This table 8 indicates that recommendations of protein intake of about 2.2-2.6 g. of protein per 100 calories can be readily supplied by a vegan diet.

Table 8: Protein Content of Selected Vegan Foods.

FOOD	AMOUNT	PROTEIN (gm)	PROTEIN (gm/100 cal)
Tempeh	1 cup	31	9.6
Soybeans, cooked	1 cup	29	9.6
Seitan	3 ounces	21	17.5
Lentils, cooked	1 cup	18	7.8
Black beans, cooked	1 cup	15	6.7
Kidney beans, cooked	1 cup	15	6.8
Chickpeas, cooked	1 cup	15	5.4
Pinto beans, cooked	1 cup	15	6.3
Lima beans, cooked	1 cup	15	6.8
Black-eyed peas, cooked	1 cup	13	6.7
Veggie burger	1 patty	13	18.6
Veggie baked beans	1 cup	12	5.0
Tofu, firm	4 ounces	11	10.6
Tofu, regular	4 ounces	10	10.7
Bagel	One (3.5 oz)	10	3.9
Quinoa, cooked	1 cup	8	3.7
Peas, cooked	1 cup	8	6.6
Textured Vegetable Protein (TVP), cooked	½ cup	8	15.0
Peanut butter	2 Tbsp	8	4.1
Veggie dog	1 link	8	13.3
Spaghetti, cooked	1 cup	8	3.7
Almonds	¼ cup	8	3.7
Soy milk, commercial,	1 cup	7	7.0
Whole wheat bread	2 slices	7	5.2

Almond butter	2 Tbsp	7	3.4
Soy yogurt, plain	8 ounces	6	4.0
Bulgur, cooked	1 cup	6	3.7
Sunflower seeds	¼ cup	6	3.3
Cashews	¼ cup	5	2.7
Spinach, cooked	1 cup	5	13.0
Broccoli, cooked	1 cup	4	6.7

Sources: USDA Nutrient Database for Standard Reference, Release 24, 2011 and manufacturer's information. The recommendation for protein for adult male vegans is around 63 grams per day; for adult female vegans it is around 52 grams per day.

Healthy dietary inclusion involves the use of unrefined grains, legumes, seeds and nuts, in order that complementarity of protein intake occurs. This concept was advocated in great detail by Frances Moore, Lappe (Diet for a Small Planet 1971 and 1982) where combining food low in one amino acid can benefit from the addition of a food high in the amino acid (complementary proteins).

PROTEIN METABOLISM

The carbon skeletons of amino acids can be catabolized to glucose and fatty acid derivatives. Overall, about 58% of ingested protein can be converted into glucose. Specific glucogenic cycles of metabolism include the alanine cycle or the urea producing ornithine cycle. Protein synthesis requires all essential amino acids to be present and under some circumstances an adequate supply of conditionally essential amino acids is required. Transamination is an important process in amino acid synthesis that depends on the availability of carbon skeletons and amino groups from many amino compounds (amino groups). Protein synthesis is controlled by the presence of DNA (deoxyribonucleic acid) and it requires the supply of energy in the form of nucleotide ATP (adenosine triphosphate).

HORMONES AND PROTEIN SYNTHESIS

It is important to note that hormonal secretions play a significant role in protein metabolism (Table 9).

HORMONE	ROLE IN PROTEIN SYNTHESIS
GROWTH HORMONE	Stimulates protein synthesis.
INSULIN	Stimulates protein synthesis by facilitating amino acid transport across cell membranes. Insulin lack reduces protein synthesis.
TESTOSTERONE	Facilitates gluconeogenesis and ketogenesis from proteins.
THYROXINE	Increases the rate of anabolism and catabolism of proteins.

Table 9: Examples of hormonal effects on protein handling by the body.

Human growth hormone (HGH) can be released by the administration of a number of amino acids (Arginine, Lysine, and Ornithine). While the release of HGH is stimulated by the infusion of several amino acids, the response to oral intake of amino acids is more variable. The presence of HGH stimulates the synthesis of insulin-like growth factor that has a trophic (growth) effect, especially on muscle tissue. Furthermore, the provision of a comprehensive array of essential amino acids in the diet or with protein supplementation can result in protein synthesis in muscles. That said, some doubt exists whether or not the enhanced synthesis of protein, by this approach, results in better exercise performance.

A number of studies have failed to show clear-cut ergogenic effects of individual amino acids or combination amino acid products such as arginine together with ornithine or lysine. Some detailed observations in individuals involved in active weight lifting have failed to show significant effects of arginine and lysine supplementation on measures of strength and body composition or any significant or sustained effects on HGH secretion. Furthermore, it is overlooked in some cases that increases in growth hormone availability do not have a consistent or sustained positive ergogenic effect in certain subjects.

A body of literature espouses the benefits of supplementation with branched chain amino acids (BCAA). It is recognized that BCAA may exert several beneficial effects on exercise performance. These effects include: support of neurotransmitter functions in the central nervous system, use as energy sources during exercise, conservation of muscle glycogen, and reductions in protein loss from muscle tissue. Much discussion and debate have occurred about the "central fatigue hypothesis," which relates high levels of free tryptophan, associated with low levels of BCAA, to the occurrence of fatigue during endurance exercise.

PROTEIN DEFICIENCIES AND MALNUTRITION

Protein energy malnutrition (PEM) include states of marasmus (energy deficiency), kwashiorkor (protein deficiency), or combinations of the two states (marasmic kwashiorkor). Varying degrees of protein or energy deficiency in the diet are often accompanied by mixed nutritional deficiencies. Often there are other stressors in the presence of marasmus or kwashiorkor, such as immune deficiency and infections. In developed nations, PEM is most often encountered secondary to chronic disease, trauma, medical treatments, or psychiatric disease.

ASSESSING THE QUALITY OF PROTEINS

Many different techniques have been used to measure the quality of various proteins in laboratory animals and humans. One simple technique is to measure protein efficiency ratios (PER). This direct technique involves the recording of weight gain in a growing animal divided by the total protein intake over a study period.

Nitrogen balance techniques can be used to determine the biological value (BV) of a protein, where measurements are made of absorbed nitrogen that is retained by the body for maintenance or growth. In addition, net protein utilization can be used to compare nitrogen intake over a period of time by examining the total nitrogen content of the animal carcass.

Measures of protein digestibility have been calculated for various foods and expressed as true digestibility or digestibility relative to reference proteins. In summary, protein quality in various foods is estimated by specific values, which include protein efficiency ratio (PER), biological value (BV), protein digestibility corrected amino scores (PDCAAS) and the more recently favored digestible indispensable amino acid scores (DIAAS).

PDCAAS AND DIAAS

The PDCAAS measures protein-containing foods based on the presence of nine essential amino acids that are adjusted for their digestibility. In addition, the Food and Agriculture Organization of the United Nations has defined amino acid requirement patterns based on the requirements of indispensable amino acids for each human age group. This recommended pattern of amino acid requirements can be used as a comparative standard to assess the quality of various food proteins and protein mixtures by calculating amino acid scores using the following equation: Amino acid score = milligrams of IDAA (indispensable amino acids) per gram of test protein divided by milligrams of IDAA per gram of reference protein, where IDAA is equal to the presence of indispensable amino acids. In these calculations, the amino acid with the lowest score is defined as the limiting amino acid. Only threonine, lysine, tryptophan, and methionine plus cysteine need to be calculated, because one or more of these amino acids is often the "limiting amino acid" in foods.

As far as protein quality is concerned, the PDCAAS has been until recently the preferred way of assessing protein quality. The highest PDCAAS score possible is 1.0. Egg whites, whey protein, casein (milk protein), and soy protein have a PDCAAS score of 1.0 and beef protein is scored at 0.92. In contrast, soybeans have a PCAACS scored at 0.91, with rice protein at 0.55 and whole wheat at 0.40. Table 10 provides examples of the PDCAAS of certain foods.

FOOD	PDCAAS
Casein	1.00
Egg white	1.00
Soybean isolate	0.99
Beef	0.92

Pea flour	0.69
Kidney beans	0.68
Chick peas	0.66
Pinto beans	0.66
Rolled oats	0.57
Lentils	0.52
Peanuts	0.52
Whole wheat	0.40

Table 10. The protein digestibility – corrected amino acid score (PDCAAS) of certain foods (source Whitney E, Rolfes S R, Understanding Nutrition 3rd edition, Thomson (Wadsworth) 2005).

The PDCAAS score of protein quality has disadvantages and limitations. This method of protein quality measurement is considered incomplete because the human diet seldom contains only one type of protein and one particular origin of protein may contain many amino acids. These circumstances make the PDCAAS higher than that of individual constituent proteins. The PDCAAS score was a standard that was used by the U.S. Food and Drug Administration following recommendations by the Food and Agricultural Organization (FAO) in 1989. While dietary proteins with a PDCAAS score of one meet all essential amino acid requirements for humans, this score has been replaced by the Digestible Indispensable Amino Acid Score (DIAAS) which was endorsed by the FAO in 2013.

The DIAAS measures provide a more accurate description of how a specific dietary source can provide human nutritional requirements for protein and amino acids. Recommendations to use the DIAAS method over the PDCAAS have occurred because DIAAS is considered a more accurate measure of amino acid digestibility in the small intestine rather than using corrected estimates of protein contents of fecal matter. Furthermore, the PDCAAS tends to overestimate plant protein availability which may contain anti-nutritional factors, e.g. soybeans and other plant proteins.

While the DIAAS method of measuring protein quality favors protein of dairy origin, the substantial levels of certain amino acids in some plant proteins (e.g. leucine and arginine in rice protein) supports their use as more premium sources of protein.

PROTEIN SUPPLEMENTS

Arguments in favor and against the use of protein supplements prevail among many nutritionists. Most individuals in Western society and industrialized societies obtain enough or surplus protein in their diet. While much interest has focused on the quality of protein or its completeness of the content of essential amino acids, proteins of plant and animal origin are most often consumed together. The ingested protein is converted during the overall digestive process into amino acids. This means that most mixed Western diets produce a pool of amino acids that is adequate to fulfill body functions.

There are a number of reasons why individuals take protein supplements in the presence of adequate protein intake. The induction of satiety by protein supplements is perceived by some individuals to be an advantage for weight control and many people use extra dietary protein as a way of repairing muscle tissue after exercise. In this context, protein is supplemented with the belief that it will cause muscle building, but, as discussed earlier, exercise exerts more effects on bodybuilding than most nutritional interventions.

Protein supplements are usually made available in three different forms, namely: protein isolate, protein hydrolysate and protein concentrate. Protein isolates are purified to produce up to 98% protein. They contain only small amounts of oils or byproducts and they are the most processed form of protein supplements. Protein concentrates are simply condensed protein and are the least processed form of supplements. In contrast, protein hydrolysates are treated with water and sometimes acids. This results in the cleavage of proteins as a consequence of chemical or enzymatic activity. Major components of protein hydrolysates are peptides and free amino acids.

There are many sources of plant protein that are reviewed in this book (Table 11).

PROTEIN TYPE	COMMENT
Sprouted Brown Rice Protein	Rice is sprouted by soaking in water to produce a type of hydrolysate. It has a smooth texture.
Soy Protein	Much concern is expressed concerning the genetic modification (GMO) of soybeans but no adverse health consequences are clearly applied to GMO-forms.
Hemp Protein	Readily available in organic form with a gritty texture and good amino acid profile.
Pea Protein	Enjoying increasing use in human and animal food with cost advantages. Variable contents of anti-nutrients e.g. phytic acid.
Other Proteins	Other interesting sources are emerging such as Chia, Sacha, Inchi, Fava bean, etc. Wheat or corn protein are very common staples in the diet.

Table 11: Selected plant proteins with general comments.

CONCEPTS OF SLOW AND FAST PROTEINS

Digestion of protein can occur in a relatively slow manner with sustainable blood levels of amino acids (e.g. rice protein) or it can occur with fast and more transient levels of amino acid concentrations in the blood (e.g. whey protein). Arguably, certain plant proteins, such as rice protein, are best described as intermediate between fast and slow proteins. This occurs in part, a consequence of different effects on the rate at which gastric emptying occurs. Proteins can induce rises in blood insulin (an insulinemic response) which are more pronounced with whey protein. Whey protein, in general, has a higher glycemic response than rice protein (rise in blood sugar).

As mentioned earlier, many diets contain mixtures of protein which act in a complementary manner. In developed countries, mixtures of sources of animal and vegetable or plant proteins are often sufficient enough in their content of indispensable or essential amino acids. In general, more total protein intake is necessary in a vegetable protein diet than in a mixed diet containing animal, fish, or egg protein. This is due to the simple fact that greater amounts of lower quality proteins, found in vegetables or plants, are required to meet obligatory requirements of amino acids and total nitrogen intake. More total protein intake of plant proteins may sometimes result in higher calorie intake. This is likely to occur when starch is associated with the selected protein origin e.g. maize.

TYPES OF PROTEIN IN CEREALS

While carbohydrates are the most common macronutrients in cereals, protein is present in concentrations of approximately 7-14% of wheat, rice, maize, oats, rye and barley. The most ubiquitous amino acid components of cereal protein are glutamine, proline and glycine. These amino acids combine with others to form albumin, globulin, glutelin and prolamin forms of protein.

Glutelins are acid soluble and when present with gliadin they form gluten. Gluten is the culprit in the cause of celiac disease (gluten enteropathy), but glutelins as a group of proteins are particularly common in rice and are referred to as oryzenin. Prolamins can be classified on their solubility characteristics into hordeins, secalins and gliadins, but more modern classifications are based on sulphur content or molecular weight. Albumins and globulins are water and saline soluble. These proteins vary significantly in amounts among different cereal types.

PROTEIN COMBINED WITH EXERCISE

Protein is only a minor source of energy in a resting individual (<5%). Using a variety of experimental methods, researchers have investigated the outcome of the use of protein during various forms of exercise (resistance training and aerobic exercise). Resistance training has been shown to have limited effects on protein or amino acid oxidation, but it appears to provoke short-term breakdown of muscle tissue.

The use of protein supplementation is quite common in individuals undergoing prolonged aerobic exercise, especially among bodybuilders. While protein assists in the production of ATP (energy stores) in muscle tissue, the rate of production of these energy resources is slower than that experienced with adequate carbohydrate and fat intake. Furthermore, sustained exercise, as mentioned earlier, will tend to promote amino acid oxidation, especially oxidation of branched chain amino acids (BCAA).

With very intense exercise there is a loss of muscle protein as a consequence of increased catabolism and/or decreased protein synthesis. A depletion of carbohydrate stores during heavy exercise results in gluconeogenesis from amino acids derived from body protein. Small amounts of protein may be lost in the urine (proteinuria), sweat and gastrointestinal tract during heavy exercise. Some studies have shown that high carbohydrate diets have protein sparing effects in athletes.

Several studies indicate that protein metabolism becomes more efficient after exercise training, mainly as a result of general adaptation. Breakdown of body protein with exercise appears to be significantly lower in the trained and conditioned athlete. As noted earlier, amino acid (BCAA) oxidation can increase during sustained exercise, but there is a trend in the presence of exercise-induced fitness to decrease the enzymatic oxidation of BCAA.

Following repeated resistance or endurance training protein balance often becomes positive. Several factors operate to increase muscle performance following training, including promotion of the synthesis of contractile muscle proteins and efficiency of oxygen utilization in the body. There is much evidence that aerobic endurance training improves the utilization of carbohydrate and fat as energy sources during exercise. It has been postulated that exercise increases the ability of muscle to derive energy from protein.

Certain studies have suggested that excessive training (sometimes resulting in over-training syndrome) exerts a negative effect, as a consequence of decreases in circulating amino acids (e.g. glutamine). The desired outcome of positive protein or nitrogen balance from training depends on an adequate supply of protein and calories. These findings support a revision upwards of the RDA of protein in the athletic adult.

Several bodies of opinion (the American Dietetic Association and American College of Sports Medicine) have recommended increases above standard recommendations of protein intake in highly active individuals. It has been proposed that individuals involved in resistance training require 1.6 to 1.7 grams of protein per kilogram of body weight, whereas those undertaking endurance exercise require an RDA of 1.2 to 1.4 grams of protein per kilogram of body weight per day, or higher. General agreement on these issues is not present. For example, the National Academy of Sciences has not recommended definitive increases in daily protein intake in endurance or resistance athletes.

Even more polar differences of opinion exist. A minority opinion exists to reduce protein intake with exercise. Some contrarian recommendations for less protein intake exist in active training adults because exercise may tend to retain protein in the later recovery periods after exercise. However, there is a general consensus opinion that the healthy athlete of normal body weight must consume enough calories and protein to maintain a healthy body weight.

Melvin H. Williams (Williams M.H., Nutrition for Health, Fitness and Sport, 8th Edition, McGraw Hill, NY, NY, 2007) has produced an excellent review of protein and other nutrient uses in adults. Williams (ibid, 2007) has made an authoritative list of general recommendations relative to dietary protein intake for athletes. This information is summarized below (Williams ibid, 2007):

- *It is recommended that all athletes obtain at least the RDA of 0.8 to 1.0 gram of protein per kilogram of body weight per day.*

- *Increases in protein should be compatible approximately with AMDR guidelines, with an increase of protein intake (RDA) in very heavy exercise by a factor of 50 to 100%.*
- *It is recommended to obtain about 15% of daily energy needs from protein. Adequate energy intake will improve protein balance and it is recommended to be taken largely in the form of carbohydrates e.g. average calorie intake for young adults is up to 3,000 calories per day and this can be adjusted upwards to about 3,500 to 4,000 calories per day.*
- *Protein consumption with adequate carbohydrate intake is recommended before and after periods of training. It is known that amino acid intake after exercise promotes muscle protein synthesis as a consequence of increasing amino acid transport. Some experimental data supports the use of taking extra nutrients prior to exercise with a view to meeting energy needs and reducing catabolic events. It has been proposed that mixtures of essential amino acids and carbohydrates can stimulate muscle protein synthesis when taken before rather than after exercise.*
- *Arguments prevail on the need for extra protein in individuals with heavy exercise.*

Overall, a high intake of protein has no adverse effects in the short term in healthy adults, but there is no convincing evidence that benefits occur as a consequence of protein intake daily in excess of 2 to 3 grams per kilogram of body weight. That said, an increase in dietary protein intake may arguably promote muscle hypertrophy, which is a desired outcome for many exercise enthusiasts.

The debate concerning the advisability of high protein diets or specific protein supplements continues in the medical literature. Several fitness experts have espoused the value of high quality protein sources such as powdered protein sources, high energy drinks combining carbohydrate and protein, sports bars, or many other combination products. Such combination products may include the addition of certain ergogenic aids.

Sports or dietary supplements are a convenient choice for individuals who may not have enough disposable time to food shop or control their diet in a meticulous manner. I believe that individuals involved in heavy exercise need protein supplementation combined with adequate calorie intake (preferably complex carbohydrates), but more convincing evidence about the ergogenic potential of protein supplementation is required.

Research studies have shown that additional body weight acquired by increasing protein intake from ranges of 0.8 to 1.4 grams per kilogram of body weight per day to 1.6 to 2.8 grams per kilogram often contributes to lean body mass. While protein balance can be maintained, in an inconsistent manner by normal protein intake (0.8 gm/kg/day or thereabouts), positive protein balance is generally higher with extra protein consumption. Several other studies have not confirmed these positive results of extra protein consumption on muscle mass, or energy or strength gains. Furthermore, there is only questionable evidence that high protein intakes can improve measures of body strength. Contrarian findings exist on the relative benefits of extra protein intake on recovering muscle damage during exercise. The jury remains out!

HIGH PROTEIN INTAKE

Evidence is still emerging that a plant protein-based diet has major health advantages, compared with an enriched animal protein diet. No authoritative advisory boards or organizations in the US have made completely clear recommendations of upper limits of protein intake, but it is advised, as suggested earlier, that daily energy intake from protein in the diet should be limited generally overall to about 35% of the total energy intake (as advised by AMDR guidelines). The National Academy of Sciences has cautioned that excessive protein intake may be related to the causation of some chronic diseases, but these recommendations refer largely to protein of animal sources.

Upon review, it is clear that estimates for protein intake do vary in a substantial manner. More than 70% of the dietary intake of protein in the U.S. and Canada originates in meat, poultry, fish, and dairy products, with average intakes of 70-100 grams of protein per day in men and 55-62 grams per day in women. A decreased amount of saturated fat and increased concentration of certain phytochemicals in plant-based whole proteins present certain health benefits that are described in several subsequent sections of this book. In brief, the potential benefits of plant proteins are apparent in reductions of body weight, cardiovascular disease (particularly atherosclerosis), certain types of cancer (especially colon cancer, prostate and breast cancer) and osteoporosis.

It has been reported that excessive protein intake may "stress" liver and kidney function due to the production of excessive urea, a tendency to acid shifts in blood pH, and ketone formation. These circumstances have led to recommendations not to take excessive protein in certain disease circumstances such as the presence of liver or kidney diseases, renal stones or diabetes mellitus. Excessive calcium loss from bones may occur in states of minor or protracted acidosis that are associated with excessive animal protein intake. Plant proteins have less of a propensity to cause these metabolic effects compared with animal protein, but adequate protein and calcium intake are mandatory to promote healthy bones and reduce fracture risks.

More research is required to examine the general health and ergonomic properties of individual amino acids in dietary supplements used by sports enthusiasts. It has been argued that significant amounts in amino acids in supplements have poorly documented intermediate to long term effects and some have specific pharmacological actions (e.g. the use of arginine to increase human growth hormone levels). Amino acid mixtures have been proposed as agents to alter neurological function, e.g. treatment of depression, but their efficacy remains in doubt and tachyphylaxis may occur. Overall, the safety or efficacy of specific isolated amino acid supplements requires further definition.

GENETIC MODIFICATION OF PLANT PROTEIN

There has been a constant search for ways to improve crop yields by the application of genetic engineering. Transfer of genes that provide resistance to plant disease and the toxic effects of weed-killers have been popular approaches, but much research is underway to improve the amino acid profile of plant proteins. Genetic modification techniques involve the transfer of genes to selected plants which can be used to encode information to increase amounts of limiting proteins in plants. Genes are transferred often from other species to donate a desired characteristic to a plant. Among the most desirable amino acids for inclusion or enrichment in plant proteins are methionine and lysine.

Among the most genetically manipulated plants are maize and varieties of corn. One highly successful protein enrichment has been the encoding of the protein zein by a gene contained within maize. Zein encoding in soybeans has been found to increase methionine content in transgenic soybeans to concentrations over 80 percent. Genetic modification of rice protein by the use of an "antisense gene" has been achieved in mice, with the objective of reducing contents of allergenic proteins in rice (Tada et al, 1996 FEBS, Letter, 391, 341-345). In addition, the valuable complete protein beta-casein can be produced by transgenic manipulations of plants. This maneuver has permitted the avoidance of bovine, milk-protein intolerance.

Similar strategies of transgenic manipulation of fruit have been used to produce sweeter, low calorie fruit or vegetables. For example, the production of the sweet protein thaumatin has been induced in potatoes and cucumber using an isolated and sequenced gene (Edens et al 1982, Gene, 18, 1-12, Witty and Harvery 1990, N.Z.J. Crop.Hort. Science 18, 77-80, Szwacka et al, 1996, Genet.Pol.37A, 58).

CONCLUSION

Expert opinions on protein intake requirements vary with variable needs under variable circumstances. Plant protein intake has many health benefits in comparison with animal protein-rich diets.

CHAPTER 1 PROTEIN: GENERAL CONSIDERATIONS

Abcouwer, S.F., and Souba, W.W. 1999. Glutamine and arginine. In Modern Nutrition in Health and Disease, eds. M. Shils, et al. Baltimore: Williams & Wilkins.

American Dietetic Association, 1997, Vegetarian Diets: Position of the ADA. Journal of the American Dietetic Association 97:1317-21.

Anderson, J., et al. 1995. Meta-analysis of the effects of soy protein intake on serum lipids. New England Journal of Medicine 333:276-82.

Antonio, J., and Street C. 1999. Glutamine: A potentially useful supplement for athletes. Canadian Journal of Applied Physiology 24:1-14.

Blomstrand, E. 2001. Amino acids and central fatigue. Amino Acids 20:25-34.

Bonjour, J., et al. 2000. Protein intake and bone growth. Canadian Journal of Applied Physiology. 26:S153-66.

Budgett, R., et al. 1998. The overtraining syndrome. In Oxford Textbook of Sports Medicine, eds. M. Harries, et al. Oxford: Oxford University Press.

Butterfield, G. 1991. Amino acids and high protein diets. In Perspectives in Exercise Science and Sports Medicine. Ergogenics: Enhancement of Sports Performance, eds. D. Lamb and M. Williams. Indianapolis, IN: Benchmark Press.

Casey, A., and Greenhaff, P. 2000. Does dietary creatine supplementation play a role in skeletal muscle metabolism and performance? American Journal of Clinical Nutrition 72:607S-17S.

Castell, L. 2003. Glutamine supplementation in vitro and in vivo, in exercise and in immunodepression. Sports Medicine 33:323-45.

Chromiak, J., and Antonio, J. 2002. Use of amino acids as growth-hormone releasing agents by athletes. Nutrition 18:657-61.

Clarkson, T. 2002. Soy, soy phytoestrogens and cardiovascular disease. Journal of Nutrition 132:566S-69S.

Consumers Union. 2001. How much protein is enough? Consumer Reports on Health 13(2):8-10.

Davis, J.M. 2000. Nutrition, neurotransmitters and central nervous system fatigue. In Nutrition in Sport, ed. R.J. Maughan. Oxford: Blackwell Science.

Davis, J.M. 1996. Carbohydrates, branched-chain amino acids and endurance: The central fatigue hypothesis. Sports Science Exchange 9 (2): 1-5.

Dawson-Hughes, B., and Harris, S. 2002. Calcium intake influences the association of protein intake with rates of bone loss in elderly men and women. American Journal of Clinical Nutrition 75:773-79.

DiPasquale, M.D. 2000. Proteins and amino acids in exercise and sport. In Energy-yielding Macronutrients & Energy Metabolism in Sports Nutrition, eds. J.A. Driskell and I. Wolinsky. Boca Raton, FL: CRC Press.

Driskell, J.A., and Wolinsky, I. 2000. Energy-yielding Macronutrients & Energy Metabolism in Sports Nutrition. Boca Raton, FL: CRC Press.

Eisenstein, J., et al. 2002. High-protein weight-loss diets: Are they safe and do they work? A review of the experimental and epidemiologic data. Nutrition Reviews 60:189-200.

Evans, W. 2001. Protein nutrition and resistance exercise. Canadian Journal of Applied Physiology 26:S141-52.

Fielding, R., and Parkington, J. 2002. What are the dietary protein requirements of physically active individuals? New evidence on the effects of exercise on protein utilization during post-exercise recovery. Nutrition in Clinical Care 5:191-96.

Fitts, R., and Metzger, J. 1993. Mechanisms of muscular fatigue. In Principles of Exercise Biochemistry, ed J. Poortmans. Basel, Switzerland: Karger.

Gibala, M. 2002. Dietary protein, amino acid supplements, and recovery from exercise. Sports Science Exchange 15 (4):1-4.

Hargreaves, M., and Snow, R. 2001. Amino acids and endurance exercise. International Journal of Sport Nutrition and Exercise Metabolism 11:133-45.

Ivy, J., and Portman, R. 2004. Nutrient Timing- The Future of Sports Nutrition. North Bergen, NJ: Basic Health Publications.

Jacobson, B. 1990. Effects of amino acids on growth hormone release. Physician and Sports medicine 18 (January): 63-70.

Krall, E.A., and Dawson-Hughes, B. 1999. Osteoporosis. In Modern Nutrition in Health and Disease, eds. M. Shils, et al. Baltimore: Williams and Wilkins.

Lawrence, M., and Kirby, D. 2002. Nutrition and sports supplements: Fact or fiction? Journal of Clinical Gastroenterology 35:299-306.

Lemon, P.W. 2000. Protein metabolism during exercise. In Exercise and Sport Science, eds. W.E. Garrett and D.T. Kirkendall. Philadelphia: Lippincott Williams & Wilkins.

Lemon, P.W. 1998. Effects of exercise on dietary protein requirements. International Journal of Sport Nutrition, 8:426-47.

Lesourd, B. 1995. Protein undernutrition as the major cause of decreased immune function in the elderly: Clinical and functional implications. Nutrition Reviews 53:S86-S94.

Mathews, D.E. 2006. Proteins and amino acids. In Modern Nutrition in Health and Disease, eds. M. Shils, et al. Philadelphia: Lippincott Williams & Wilkins.

Messina, V.K., and Burke, K.I. 1997. Position of the American Dietetic Association: Vegetarian diets. Journal of the American Dietetic Association 97:1317-21.

Millward, D. 2004. Macronutrient intakes as determinants of dietary protein and amino acid adequacy. Journal of Nutrition 134:1588S-96S.

National Academy of Sciences. 2002. Dietary Reference Intakes for Energy, Carbohydrates, Fiber, Fat, Protein and Amino Acids (Macronutrients). Washington, DC: National Academies Press.

Nieman, D. 2001. Exercise immunology: Nutrition countermeasures. Canadian Journal of Applied Physiology 26:S45-55.

Parkhouse, W. 1988. Regulation of skeletal muscle myofibrillar protein degradation: Relationships to fatigue and exercise. International Journal of Biochemistry 20:769-75.

Phillips, S. 2004. Protein requirements and supplementation in strength sports. Nutrition 20:689-95.

Poortmans, J. 1993. Protein metabolism. In Principles of Exercise Biochemistry, ed. J. Poortmans. Basel, Switzerland: Karger.

Rennie, M. 2001. Control of muscle protein synthesis as a result of contractile activity and amino acid availability: Implications for protein requirements. International Journal of Sport Nutrition and Exercise Metabolism 11:S170-76.

Rennie, M., and Tipton, K. 2000. Protein and amino acid metabolism during and after exercise and the effects of nutrition. Annual Review of Nutrition 20:457-83.

Slater, G., and Jenkins, D. 2000. Beta-hydroxy-beta-methylbutyrate (HMB) supplementation and the promotion of muscle growth and strength. Sports Medicine 30:105-16.

Tarnopolsky, M. 2004. Protein requirements for endurance athletes. Nutrition. 20:662-68.

Tipton, K., and Wolfe, R. 2004. Protein and amino acids for athletes. Journal of Sports Sciences 22:65-79.

Tipton, K., and Wolfe, R.R. 1998. Exercise-induced changes in protein metabolism. Acta Physiologica Scandinavica 162: 377-87.

Wagenmakers, A. 2000. Amino acid metabolism in exercise. In Nutrition in Sport, ed.

Wagenmakers, A. 1997. Branched-chain amino acids and endurance performance. In The Clinical Pharmacology of Sport and Exercise, eds. T. Reilly and M. Orme. Amsterdam: Elsevier Science BV.

Walberg-Rankin, J.W. 1999. Role of protein in exercise. Clinics in Sports Medicine 18:499-511.

Williams, M.H. 1999. Facts and fallacies of purported ergogenic amino acid supplements. Clinics in Sports Medicine 18:633-49.

Wolfe, R. 2001. Effects of amino acid intake on anabolic processes. Canadian Journal of Applied Physiology 26:S220-27.

Wolfe, R. 2000. Protein supplements and exercise. American Journal of Clinical Nutrition 72:551S-557S.

Yoshimura, H. 1970. Anemia during physical training (sports anemia). Nutrition Review 28:251-53.

CHAPTER 2
SWITCHING TO PLANT PROTEIN DIETS

SWITCHING TO PLANT PROTEIN DIETS

Foundations for a switch from animal to vegetable or other plant-based diets involve the recognition that correct, mixed plant intakes are adequate in their nutritional content. Moreover, diets of plant origin confer health benefits with disease prevention properties. The key characteristic of a healthy vegetarian diet is the correct use of mixed plant intake that will provide adequate nutrition. This means the avoidance of deficiencies in calorie, vitamin, minerals, and macronutrient intake, especially in relationship to protein intake. Protein intake is not omnipotent for health when taken alone.

It is clear that to achieve a sufficient intake of essential amino acids from a vegetarian diet, it is necessary to eat plant foods that contain complementary proteins. One important balance of essential amino acids comes from combining grains and cereals with legumes. As noted, low lysine-containing cereals or grains can be complemented by higher lysine containing legumes. Also, legumes can be low in methionine and this can be complemented by high concentration of this amino acid in grain products.

There are "degrees" of vegetarianism ranging from complete absence of all animal protein in the diet through partial animal protein inclusion. Vegans eat no animal protein, whereas ovo-vegetarians and lacto-vegetarians permit the inclusion of eggs and milk products, respectively. Semi-vegetarians exist with the dietary exclusion of meat, beef and pork products, but the inclusion of fish and poultry. Fish-consumers who avoid poultry and other meats are referred to as pesco-vegetarians.

It is notable that many population studies show that vegetarian diets are associated with a lower prevalence of certain chronic diseases including hypertension, obesity, strokes, heart disease, and certain types of cancer. Most causes of mortality are reduced by switching to vegetarian (fruit, vegetable and other plant intake). Plant based diets are healthful because they are low in saturated fat and cholesterol intake, high in dietary fiber and low in calories. In addition, plant based diets are high in vitamins and minerals, as well as provide a valuable source of antioxidant compounds and other health-giving phytochemicals (Table 12).

PHYTOCHEMICALS	COMMON PLANT SOURCES
Allium sulfides:	Garlic
	Onions
Anthocyanins	Blueberries
Capsaicin	Hot peppers
Carotenoids:	Carrots
Beta-carotene	Dark-green leafy vegetables
Lycopene	Sweet potatoes
Lutein	Tomatoes
Flavonoids:	Citrus fruits
Quercetin	Broccoli
Indoles:	Cruciferous vegetables
	Broccoli
	Brussel sprouts
	Cabbage
	Cauliflower
	Kale
Isoflavones:	Soybeans
Phytoestrogens	Peanuts
Genistein	Soy milk
Isothiocyanates:	Cruciferous vegetables
Sulforaphane	Broccoli

		Brussel sprouts
		Cabbage
		Cauliflower
		Kale
Phenolic acids:		Carrots
		Citrus fruits
		Tomatoes
		Whole grains
Polyphenols:		Grapes
Resveratrol		Green tea
		Wine
Saponins:		Beans
		Legumes
Terpenes:		Cherries
Limonene		Citrus fruits

Table 12: Phytochemicals found in common food sources.

It is noted earlier that plant proteins are variably deficient in certain amino acids, the most significant of which is lysine. This circumstance has led experts in vegan nutrition to recommend a search for higher lysine content in plant proteins. Notable lysine-containing plant proteins are found in several legumes, quinoa, seitan, pistachios and pumpkin seeds. Overall, legumes tend to be low in their content of methionine and other plant proteins tend to be low in lysine. It is recognized that those individuals who meet lysine requirements on a vegan diet are usually meeting overall protein needs.

Protein requirements in vegans need further study and definition. There have been a handful of key nitrogen balance studies in people consuming a vegan diet following a switch from regular diets. It has been estimated that vegans may benefit from a dietary intake of protein in the range of 1.0-1.1 grams per day, but recommendations have been made for more nitrogen balance studies on practicing vegans.

PLANT PROTEIN DIETS CONFER HEALTH ADVANTAGES

This book points to a plethora of information in medical literature which reaches overall conclusions that switching from animal to plant protein-containing diets may improve health. A recent study has linked high levels of animal protein consumption in individuals under 65 years with risks of premature death (Levine, M.E., et al Low Protein Intake Is Associated with a Major Reduction in IGF, Cancer, and Overall Mortality in the 65 and Younger but Not Older Population, Cell Metabolism, 19, 407-417, 2014).

In these studies (Levine et al ibid, 2014) it is striking that the risks of premature death were considerably less when protein was of plant origin, notably beans and vegetables. The results of this study suggested that low animal protein intake during middle age, which is followed by moderate to high protein intake in the elderly, may improve longevity. The magnitude of the negative effects of preferential animal protein intake in these studies was highly significant. There was a four fold increase in the risk of death from cancer and diabetes and nearly two times the risk of dying from any cause over an eighteen year period of study. The risks of high animal protein intake were perceived as equivalent in harm to health problems caused by smoking, but arguments have prevailed because of the many difficulties in defining the health effects of individual nutrients by controlling for other factors that determine health and longevity.

In experimental animals, growth hormone receptor deficiency or growth hormone deficiency are known to prolong lifespan and reduce age-related degenerative diseases, including cancer and diabetes. In fact, humans with growth hormone receptor deficiency have decreased levels of IGF-1. These individuals have reduced cancer mortality and a lower prevalence of diabetes (Levine M. E., et al, ibid, 2014).

The dietary restriction of certain amino acids (methionine and tryptophan) may explain the effect, at least in part, on enhancing longevity and certain chronic disease risk. This dietary restriction of protein may result in lower IGF-1 levels and increase longevity with a reduction in the occurrence of cancer. These effects could be independent of calorie intake and they are further examples of the effects of protein selection (or dietary composition) on disease incidence and mortality.

The results of the epidemiological study of 6,381 men and women aged 50 years and above provide understanding of the links between dietary sources and amounts of protein intake, disease incidence, mortality and aging (Levine, M.E., ibid, 2014). It is apparent that the amount of protein of animal origin consumed accounted for a large proportion of the demonstrated association of total protein intake and all causes of mortality. It seems that high levels of protein intake that cause high levels of insulin and IGF-1 may be a key cause of mortality in individuals aged 50 to 65 years of age.

These recent studies (Levine, M.E., ibid, 2014) implied that low protein intake in elderly individuals (> 65 years of age) was detrimental. It has been reasoned that elevation of IGF-1 and insulin is beneficial in older subjects where weight tends to decline and sarcopenia occurs. Elderly subjects who have lost body weight as a consequence of aging are likely to be vulnerable to protein malnourishment. Genetic factors and co-existent diseases may amplify the negative effects of protein restriction in the elderly.

In summary, the studies of Levine, M.E. (ibid, 2014) imply that a reduced protein diet in middle age may be beneficial in cancer and diabetes prevention, with a decrease in overall mortality. This phenomenon may be related to a significant degree to the changes in circulating IGF-1 and insulin levels. These findings are supported by animal experiments in mice where high protein diets cause rises in IGF-1, which results in an increased risk of cancer. Several animal experiments and population studies indicate that diets rich in plant-based foods are likely to confer major health benefits in all adults. These conclusions are supported by several pivotal studies:

- Estruch, J. et al, N. Engl. J. Med., 2013, 368 1279-1290. These studies show the importance of a Mediterranean diet in the prevention of cardiovascular disease.
- Linos, E. and Willett, W.C., J. Natl. Compr. Cancer. Netw, 2007, 5, 711-718. This study shows the benefit of plant-based diets on breast cancer reduction.
- Michaud et al, Cancer Causes Control, 2001, 12, 557-567. This study links animal protein intake to prostate cancer occurrence.
- Willett, W.C., Public Health and Nutrition, 2006, 9, 1A, 105-110. This series of observations links the Mediterranean diet with health advantages.

MEAT AND CANCER RISK

The importance of reducing meat intake to lower cancer risk is well accepted in the practice of Integrative and Nutritional Medicine. Many scientific studies link the occurrence of different types of cancer with red meat and processed meat intake. A number of carcinogenic substances are present in processed or barbequed meats. These compounds include: nitrites and nitrates, heterocyclic amines and polycyclic aromatic hydrocarbons. The presence of these substances in common meat dishes highlights the importance of diet composition on disease risk. It is increasingly recommended that individuals switch more towards plant-based protein diets to reduce the occurrence of cancer affecting several different organs including cancer of: the lung, breast, esophagus, pancreas, larynx, stomach, kidney, endometrium, ovaries and the prostate.

PLANT PROTEIN DIETS CONFER MANY HEALTH BENEFITS: FURTHER REVIEW

It is relevant to revise and discuss further the general principles of the nutritional value of proteins before the ensuing more detailed review of the main types of plant proteins in the remainder of this book. In review, the Institute of Medicine recommends 0.8 grams of protein per day, per kilogram of body weight (or about 8 grams of protein per 20 pounds of body weight).

To review the circumstance in different terms, the U.S. recommended daily protein intake for women over the age of 19 years is 46 grams and for men over 19 years of age is 56 grams. It is clear that animal protein is complete in its content of essential amino acids, but we have learned that some plant proteins are variably deficient in certain essential amino acids. This circumstance dictates the need for plant protein intake to be composed of a mixed plant diet (intentional echolalia).

High protein foods have different health consequences depending on their associated dietary constituents, e.g. concentrations of saturated fat, cholesterol, healthy unsaturated fats (e.g. omega-3 fatty acids), fiber, antinutrients, allergens and mineral components (e.g. sodium). While red meat is not only a source of damaging saturated fat and cholesterol, as mentioned earlier, it may be cooked in a manner that delivers carcinogens (e.g. charbroiled meat).

While animal protein in red meat is complete in its amino acid content, there is even more evidence that healthier sources of protein are present in fish and plant proteins, resulting in a lower incidence of several chronic diseases and early death (Bernstein, A.M., et al, Circulation, 122, 9, 876-83, 2010, Aune et al, Diabetologica, 52, 11, 2277-87, 2009, Pan et al, Arch. Int. Med., 172, 7, 555-63, 2012). I emphasize again that healthy protein choices result in a lower prevalence of cardiovascular disease, type II diabetes mellitus, osteoporosis and cancer. In general, a lower consumption of red meat can be combined with more healthy protein sources from fish, chicken and plant proteins.

It is important to distinguish both the health benefits and negative health consequences of consuming different proteins in varying amounts. In addition, it is equally important to realize that "whole food" is the common source of essential dietary protein and different foods have a variety of other constituents with different health implications. These differences become clear when examining the health benefits of certain foods that are determined by their overall nutritional content.

For example, pumpkin seeds provide about 9.35 grams of protein per ounce and they are a rich source of tryptophan and glutamate, both of which support neurotransmitter function. On the other hand, cauliflower provides about 2.28 grams of protein per cooked cup. The real health benefits of cauliflower are due to its antioxidant contents of carotenoids and phytonutrients (including kaempferol, ferulic, cinnamic, and caffeic acid). For example, sulphorane and indole 3 carbinol, found in cauliflower, are anti-carcinogenic. It is clear that different legumes and cereals have different and individual health benefits that are independent of their protein content.

T. COLIN CAMPBELL SPEAKS

T. Colin Campbell has carried several of the most important messages about protein nutrition that are present in his revered book The China Study (Ben Bella Books Inc., 2005). These messages uncover the importance of plant proteins in nutrition and their superior health-giving properties in comparison with animal protein. Dr. Campbell (The China Study ibid, 2005) implies that many years of science have shown that protein of animal origin is utilized by the body in a more efficient manner than plant protein. Moreover, animal protein promotes superior rates of growth in animals and humans, but it is not optimal for body health. Moreover, Campbell has proposed the important notion that *"food-based nutrition is far, far more important in health than nutrient-based nutrition"* (Campbell T C, nutrition studies.org/author/tcc). Dr. Campbell proposes that animal protein may increase body growth but it may cause increases in cancer cell growth, a high prevalence of heart disease, advancing of the aging process and decrease in bone mass. Moreover, he gives an example of increased rate of growth due to animal protein in girls as causing early sexual maturation with dominance of estrogen secretion and a high occurrence of breast cancer in later life (Campbell ibid, 2005 and ww.nutritionstudies.org/author/tcc/January 19, 2014).

Laboratory studies performed over a two decade period by Dr. Campbell and his colleagues have shown that the consumption of animal-based casein (principal protein in cow's milk) has a number of potentially negative outcomes. Whereas casein stimulates growth hormone in childhood, plant protein in typical whole food plant based (WFPB) diets does not result in this phenomenon to the same extent. These and other observations have led to conclusions that animal-based protein diets are of greater biological value or have higher quality than plant based diets (a matter of fact).

To reiterate, there is an excess of protein intake in the U.S. diet but recommendations exist for 0.8 gm/kg of body weight for protein, resulting in 56 grams in a 70 kg male and 48 grams in a 60 kg female. This means that approximately 10 percent protein intake per day in the diet is necessary to maintain health and comply with Recommended Daily Amount (RDA) of protein. The U.S.A. diet contains about 17 percent of protein in up to 95 percent of individuals and most of this protein is of animal origin (70-80%). Campbell T C (ibid, 2014) describes these circumstances as causing adverse health consequences including the adverse consequences of animal protein per se and the reduction of the health benefits of whole food plant-based (WFPB) diets.

There are several documented disadvantages of animal based protein on health. Table 13.

PROBLEMS WITH ANIMAL PROTEIN	COMMENT
DIETARY FAT	There is an increase in cancer rates associated with high fat diets which is attributable to animal based diets (arguments prevail).
HEART DISEASE	A clear relationship exists between animal protein (meat and dairy) with high cholesterol intake and total saturated dietary fat consumption. This results in an association of heart disease with excessive animal protein intake. Evidence exists that animal protein is more effective in increasing the early stages of atherosclerosis than dietary fat.
CANCER	A reduction in animal protein intake may be assumed to reduce the risk of

	cancer, e.g. Casein may increase the risk of hepatic cancer in animals and humans.
DIABETES MELLITUS	Meta-Analysis studies show a significant (26 percent) increase in Type-2 diabetes mellitus in association with excessive animal protein intake. Results of the Harvard Nurses Health Study indicate that animal protein intake was associated with excess mortality from cardiovascular disease and cancer.
OSTEOPOROSIS	Bone fracture rates are correlated with dietary calcium and animal protein intake. This association is likely to be related to an increased risk of osteoporosis with increased dairy intake.
GENERAL MORTALITY	Large studies or metanalyses taken in aggregate have shown that red meat (processed or unprocessed) was associated significantly with increased total mortality overall by a factor 10-44 percent with cardiovascular disease deaths of 18-28 percent and cancer mortality of 10-32 percent. Studies show that switching from meat-based diets to WFPB (whole food plant-based) diets can reverse cardiovascular disease in 90-100 percent of subjects. These observations are supported by cross-sectional studies in different countries where cancer and cardiovascular

	disease rates are lower in association with more modest intake of dietary animal fat (a marker of animal protein intake).

Table 13. The disease outcomes of animal-based protein diets (adapted from Campbell T C, www.nutritionstudies.or/author'tcc/.January 19, 2014.

FOOD FORTIFIED WITH PLANT PROTEIN

There has been a recent interest in fortified protein foods in the U.S. with a preference for inclusion of pulse products (especially dried peas, chickpeas, beans and lentils). While soy and pea protein are becoming ubiquitous ingredients in U.S. food, they are often added to granola, cereal and breakfast snacks that are typically high in fat, salt or sugar. These latter additions tend to obscure some of the health benefits of plant proteins. While protein intake is not deficient in American diets, it can increase levels of satiety and may act with benefits in obesity management and prevention. As mentioned repeatedly, excessive animal protein tends to promote cancer, cardiovascular disease, diabetes mellitus, osteoporosis and overall mortality. Protein fortification has become popular in a variety of circumstances such as additions to extra servings in fast food restaurants, biscuits and even milk. Sales of these products are expanding rapidly.

CALORIE RESTRICTION, HEALTH AND LONGEVITY

Calorie restriction (CR) in the diet, without the induction of malnutrition, has been shown to increase life span in animals in a consistent manner. The same is probably true in primates and humans, but the overall composition of the diet can exert influences on disease occurrence and longevity. For example, organochemicals found in processed or barbequed meat may be carcinogenic.

There are thousands of published articles, over an eighty year period, that focus on the ability of significant reductions in calorie intake to exert their effects on enhancing life span and reducing the incidence and prevalence of age-related diseases. Much of this literature refers to animal models of aging. It appears that the application of calorie restriction of the order of 30-50% (up to 70%) below average free-feeding calorie intake may induce an inhibitory effect on many aspects of aging, including aging processes in non-human species, primates and probably humans (a best guess).

A precise definition of the required level of calorie restriction to promote longevity is not possible, especially in these days of much "social gluttony." About a 30-40% reduction below a 2,000K cal intake in humans may suffice to promote longevity ("a hard act to follow"). Many people ingest 3,000 to 6,000 calories per day which may require about a 50-70% reduction in intake to result in any longevity benefits. Much research has been performed on calorie restriction in rodents and it appears that biological responses to calorie restriction are quite similar in primates and humans. However, one could anticipate intraindividual and interindividual responses to different levels of reductions in daily calorie intake and episodic fasting are longevity promoters that have not been studied in detail.

There are many proponents of the use of food restriction strategies for anti-aging. The first observations of the lifespan-enhancing ability of calorie-restriction were made more than 80 years ago. These observations lay somewhat dormant in the medical literature, until the 1950s, when the pioneer of modern calorie restriction interventions, Professor Roy Walford started to popularize his concepts of the "120 Year Old Diet." In brief, Walford discussed the advantage of the "high/low diet," where he suggested a combination of "under-nutrition without malnutrition for health and longevity."

The proposals of Professor Walford involved the careful application of a calorie restricted diet that was "nutrient dense." Nutrient density implies the provision of vital and essential nutritional cofactors, most notably vitamins and minerals with phytonutrients. Interests in calorie restriction have accelerated to a point where this approach has generated great interest as a research focus for the U.S. National Institutes of Aging. Recent research has expanded beyond laboratory animals to human interventions using dietary calorie restriction or substances that can mimic the biological changes that are seen in the presence of significant reductions of daily calorie intake (so-called "Calorie Restriction Mimetics").

Conservative scientists demand to see more research into the human effects of calorie restriction as an anti-aging strategy, but it seems prudent to accept this intervention as a valid, reliable and safe approach to enhancing lifespan. Governments of industrial societies have made recent calls to lower calorie intake in the diets, while many sectors of the modern food industry continue to "peddle" calorie excess.

A simple understanding of the biochemical and physiological effects of calorie restriction explains why this intervention can extend average lifespan (defined as the average number of years that an organism is expected to live). There is a major and added bonus to the intervention. Calorie restriction may also facilitate the prolongation of maximum lifespan (defined as the greatest number of years that a living organism can survive).

It is efficient, but not necessarily sufficient, to "classify" several areas of the biological outcome of calorie restriction. These areas include, but may not be limited to, the following: alteration of the expression and actions of many key enzyme systems that control body metabolism and protein synthesis, reduction of the accumulation and removal of damaged proteins, modulation of normal processes of cell death (apoptosis), modification of the actions of chaperone molecules, secondary reduction in protein/sugar cross-linking (glycosylation), variable reversal of dysglycemia (poor glucose homeostasis), reduction of chronic inflammation and inflammatory markers, hormetic effects ("good forms" of stress), inhibition of glycolysis with insulin-sensitizing actions and specific influences on genes that alter cell repair or death (e.g. Sir2 gene or the human homologous SIRT1 gene).

Table 14 is composed of line item statements of the biophysiological benefits of calorie restriction, observed in animal and some human studies:

- Favorable effects on cardiovascular structure and function, with reductions in heart rate, blood pressure, LDL cholesterol and triglycerides.

- Improvements in insulin sensitivity and overall normalization of blood glucose levels.
- Increase in protein synthesis and the elimination of abnormal proteins from the body. Enhanced action of chaperone molecules which contribute to the synthesis and maintenance of essential proteins, with the benefit of enhanced elimination of damaged proteins.
- Modulation of the process of "orderly cell death" (apoptosis), with improvement in the repair and maintenance of the integrity of DNA. Secondary benefits on transcription.
- Reduction of oxidative stress to tissues by diminution of free radical generation in a quantitative and qualitative manner.
- Reduction in body temperature.
- Reduction of body fat mass, including visceral adiposity, with concomitant increase in muscle mass.
- Beneficial effects on hormonal secretions that tend to fall with age, e.g. DHEA and growth hormone.
- Improvements in brain function, including memory, cognition and perhaps mood.
- Spontaneous enhancement of an ability to engage in physical activity.
- Stimulation of growth factors, e.g. BDNF, a nerve growth factor.
- Weight loss and its many secondary beneficial effects.

Table 14. The bio-physiological and clinical outcomes that have been described in many experiments that have utilized calorie restriction or, in some limited cases, calorie restriction mimetics.

It is noted that individuals who undertook sustained programs of calorie restriction were able to control blood glucose in a range of 74 to 88 mg/dL. Proponents of calorie restriction diets place the optimum target of a fasting blood glucose below 85 mg/dL, approximately (Fontana L, Curr Opin Gastroenterol, 25, 2, 144-50, 2009, McGlothin P, Averill M. Glucose Control: The Sweet Spot in Longevity. In: McGlothin P, Averill M. The CR Way: Using the Secrets of Calorie Restriction for a Longer, Healthier Life. New York, NY: HarperCollins; 2008: 57-78).

There is evidence that control of blood glucose within ideal ranges produces favorable metabolic changes that favor thermogenesis (fat burning) and protein utilization (Holt S, Peel off the Weight; The Holt Institute of Medicine, 2010, www.hiom.org).

CALORIE RESTRICTION AND OXIDATIVE STRESS

Calorie restriction has been shown to exert beneficial effects on lifespan by decreasing oxidative stress to tissues. In carefully conducted studies in elderly mice, the effects of calorie restricted diets that contained or generated advanced glycation and products (AGE's) were compared with standard or simple calorie restricted diets (Cai W et al, Am J. Pathol, 173, 2, 327-36, 2008). In these studies, the old mice who took the AGE's-loaded form of the calorie restricted diet developed more biomarkers of oxidative stress, (insulin resistance, cardiovascular disease, renal disorders and impaired longevity) compared with substantially similar old mice who took a simple calorie restricted diet. These observations support the notion that calorie restriction works, in part, by decreasing oxidative stress.

A plant-based diet that delivers antioxidants would be expected to amplify the benefits of calorie restriction. Thus, the quality of the calorie restricted diet is important, with the need for lower oxidative stress-inducing components. These findings reinforce the work of Roy Walford who stressed the value of using a calorie restricted diet that did not involve the induction of malnutrition. This is the concept of the high/low diet, namely calorie restriction with high vital nutrient density.

PRIMATE STUDIES ON CALORIE RESTRICTION

Primates have aging characteristics that are quite similar to humans. In a pivotal and groundbreaking series of studies on Rhesus monkeys, researchers have been able to show unequivocal evidence of the anti-aging properties of calorie restricted diets (Colman et al, Science, 325, 5937, 201-4, 2009). The studies involved two groups of monkeys, where one group was allowed to engage in free-feeding (ad libitum eating) and the other were given a nutrient dense diet that was 30% lower in calories. The monkeys were monitored for two decades with observations of the development of age-related disease, biomarkers of aging and times of death.

After 20 years, the control group of free-feeding monkeys had a 37% death rate, compared with a 13% death rate in the dietary restricted animals. Among the calorie restricted monkeys, Type II diabetes or Metabolic Syndrome X did not occur, in comparison with a 40% incidence of these disorders in the control group. Cardiovascular disease was 50% lower in calorie-restricted monkeys and lower percentages of body fat with retention of muscle mass were predictably apparent in the calorie restricted group of monkeys.

These observations in calorie restricted monkeys are paralleled by findings in humans where 20% reduction in calorie intake for up to six years results in improvements in blood cholesterol, blood pressure, weight control and glucose homeostasis (Everitt AV and Le Couteur DG, Ann. NY. Acad. Sci, 1114, 428-33, 2007). In essence, calorie restriction is a pivotal factor in correcting the constellation of problems that are found in Metabolic Syndrome X, a condition that is associated with increased death rates from all causes. Even non-sustained periods of calorie restriction may have favorable effects, such as reducing inflammation, improvements in mitochondrial function and reduction of oxidative stress to tissues etc.

CALORIE RESTRICTION WORKS IN HUMANS

Over the past decade, The National Institutes of Health have funded several studies on the results of calorie restriction in humans. Overall, the results of this research show clear health benefits. In multicenter studies, beneficial outcomes of calorie restriction have been noted in atherosclerotic cardiovascular disease, cardiac function, insulin resistance, with notable improvements in several biomarkers of aging (Fontana L et al, Proc. Natl. Acad. Sci, 101, 17, 6659-63, 2004, Meyer TE et al. J Am Coll. Cardiology, 47, 2, 3984-402, 2006 and Heilbronn LK et al, JAMA, 295, 13, 1539-48).

There is now mounting evidence that calorie restriction works in humans, in a similar manner to its effects on many animal species. The human studies show changes in biophysiological parameters similar to those observed in animals e.g. decreased fasting insulin, reduction in tissue damage from oxidative stress, decrease in body temperature etc.

The support for the use of calorie restriction interventions in longevity medicine is bolstered by experiments that involved a few (eight) scientists who followed a calorie restriction protocol for almost two years. In this study, the human volunteers exhibited similar physiological changes that were observed in primates who had been subjected to equivalent levels of calorie restriction. These are truly exciting observations which are quite compatible with information from population studies or epidemiological findings of the health benefits that result generally from the retention of a normal or low weight range. Again, the switch to a plant-based diet would act in a synergistic manner to assist in weight control, especially as a consequence of satiety induction.

INFLAMMATION AND AGING

Chronic smoldering inflammation is a major catalyst for premature aging. For example, much evidence links the occurrence of insulin resistance to underlying inflammation. Insulin resistance is the key underlying factor in the causation of the constellation of problems that constitute Metabolic Syndrome X, Prediabetes, and their progression to Type II Diabetes Mellitus. Thus, interventions that curb or suppress inflammation constitute key antiaging strategies. Inflammation is a common consequence of oxidative stress which must be dealt with, in order to prevent the development of "cascades of inflammation." This circumstance results in "obesitis" (the authors neologism to stress that obesity is in part an inflammatory disorder).

Calorie restriction has specific effects on reducing inflammation by blocking oxidative stress and inhibiting the actions or production of inflammatory mediators. This beneficial situation is often achieved by effects on genes that regulate inflammatory cascades, glucose homeostasis and blood lipids. The idea of calorie restriction remains an important and highly effective approach to anti-aging. One may focus on the fact that obesity is rapidly becoming the number one preventable cause of premature death and disability in industrialized societies and dietary calorie restrictions are very important. That said, the importance of a switch from excessive animal protein intake to correct amounts of plant protein intake will be an increasingly important factor in the promotion of longevity. This ecofriendly approach must be considered in more detail.

MEETING GLOBAL FOOD DEMANDS

Attempts to discover new ways that could ease global food and calorie demands have attracted much recent interest (Julian I et al Nature, 497 (7447), 2013:60 Do1: 10.1038/nature 11909). New studies that examine the mechanisms whereby plants transport key substances across their cell membranes have major implications for the supply of food and energy. In particular, membrane functions that enhance tolerance to droughts, control water loss from vegetation, store sugar and resist environmental toxins could lead to major improvements in global plant protein availability.

DIETARY IMPROVEMENTS 2009-2010 IN U.S.A.

Studies from the Harvard School of Public Health (HSPH) shows that there has been a trend over the decade 1999-2010 to improve the quality of food intake in the U.S.A. While there has been an appropriate reduction in trans-fat intake, it is considered that dietary habits remain inadequate and there are increasing differences among individuals of various socioeconomic and ethnic status (Dong D et al, JAMA Internal Medicine, September 1, 2014).

Changes that were responsible for improving dietary habits included: consumption of more fruit, whole grains, nuts, legumes and polyunsaturated fats with less intake of sweetened beverages. However, salt intake increased with no increase in vegetable intake and no reductions in red meat or processed meat intake. The benefits of enhanced plant protein intake are not apparent in these recent studies (Dong D et al, ibid, 2014).

HARVARD SPEAKS

The Nutrition Source of Harvard Medical School (www.hsph.harvard.ed/ nutrition source/protein-full story) writes about "Protein: Moving closer to Center Stage". The next few sections of this book summarize a point of view on protein research and its influence on common disease states. It will become apparent that several difference of opinion have emerged on the benefits of plant-based high protein diets.

There have been expressed concerns that high protein diets may cause heart disease. However, there is reason to question these fears. It seems that eating more plant protein and animal protein to a lesser degree in the presence of reduced refined carbohydrates may have cardiac benefits. Holton et al (N. Engl. J. Med, 355, 1991-2002, 2006) showed in a prospective study in 82,802 women, that those found eating less carbohydrate with high sources of fat or protein resulted in a 30 percent lower risk of heart disease, compared with women who consumed high-carbohydrate, low fat diets. However, women with low carbohydrate diets rich in animal protein or fats had no reduction in the risk of heart disease.

DIABETES MELLITUS

It has been argued that the amount of protein in the diet does not apparently affect the development of Type 2 diabetes. A study by Lee et al (Am J. Clin Nutri, 89, 1920-6, 2009) indicates that consuming a diet that is low carbohydrate with high vegetable sources of protein and fat can reduce the risk of developing Type 2 diabetes mellitus. Studies show potential benefits of plant protein and nutritional yeast in the management of diabetes compared with animal protein (beef, pork and lamb, etc.) Moreover, the best types of animal protein for health are fish and poultry protein (not red meat or pork).

OSTEOPOROSIS

The assimilation of protein by the body results in a status of body acidification which can pull calcium from bones. In the Nurses Health Study women who consumed excessive protein (greater than 95 percent of RDI per day) had a greater prevalence of wrist fractures over a 12 month period compared to women with average protein intake of less than 68 grams per day. However, inconsistent results have been found in several research projects on the relationship of osteoporosis (thin bones) and protein intake. Overall, data imply that plant protein is bone sparing in comparison with animal protein.

WEIGHT CONTROL

There is evidence in the short term that high protein, low carbohydrate diets produce accelerated weight loss. Clinical trials have confirmed that "the low carb diet" is superior in weight loss outcome to low fat diets (Foster G D et al, N. Engl. J. Med., 348, 2074-81, 2003). Why the low carb diet works with great efficiency is not clear, but it may be a function of protein causing delayed gastric emptying with satiety, a low glycemic effect of protein and the greater degree of energy required to digest protein compared with fat or carbohydrate. That said, the general consensus remains that a low carb diet could not be considered to be healthy as a long term dietary adjustment.

CONCLUSION

Research indicates that plant based diets present an option of affordable safe interventions to help lower body mass index, Hb A1C, blood pressure, cholesterol levels and the prevalence of cancer. In addition, they may help to reduce the number of medications required to treat disease and lower the prevalence of ischemic heart disease, (the number one killer).

CHAPTER 2 REFERENCES

Abelow, B. J., Holford, T. R. & Insogna, K. L. Cross-cultural association between dietary animal protein and hip fracture: a hypothesis. Calcif. Tissue Int. 50, 14-18 (1992).

Armstrong, D. & Doll, R. Environmental factors and cancer incidence and mortality in different countries, with special reference to dietary practices. Int. J. Cancer 15, 617-631 (1975).

Aune, D., Ursin, G. & Veierod, M. B. Meta-analysis. Meat consumption and the risk of type-2 diabetes: a systematic review and meta-analysis of cohort studies. Diabetolgia 52, 2277-2287 (2009).

Ayala, V., Naudi, A., Sanz, A., Caro, P., Portero-Otin, M., Barja, G., and Pamplona, R. (2007). Dietary protein restriction decreases oxidative protein damage, peroxidizability index, and mitochondrial complex I content in rat liver. J. Gerontol. A Biol. Sci. Med. Sci. 62, 352-360.

Bartali, B., Frongillo, E.A., Bandinelli, S., Lauretani, F., Semba, R.D., Fried, L.P., and Ferrucci, L. (2006). Low nutrient intake is an essential component of frailty in older persons. J. Gerontol. A Biol. Sci. Med. Sci. 61, 589-593.

Bartke, A., Brown-Borg, H., Mattison, J., Kinney, B., Hauck, S., and Wright, C. (2001). Prolonged longevity of hypopituitary dwarf mice. Exp. Gerontol. 36, 21-28.

Bellush, L.L., Doublier, S., Holland, A.N., Striker, L.J., Striker, G.E., and Kopchick, J.J. (2000). Protection against diabetes-induced nephropathy in growth hormone receptor/binding protein gene-disrupted mice. Endocrinology 141, 163-168.

Blanton, C.A., Moshfegh, A.J., Baer, J.D., and Kretsch, M.J. (2006). The USDA Automated Multiple-Pass Method accurately estimates group total energy and nutrient intake. J. Nutr. 136, 2594-2599.

Boirie, Y., Gachon, P., and Beaufrere, B. (1997). Splanchnic and whole-body leucine kinetics in young and elderly men. Am. J. Clin. Nutr. 65, 489-495.

Brown-Borg, H.M., and Bartke, A. (2012). GH and IGF1: roles in energy metabolism of long-living GH mutant mice. J. Gerontol. A Biol. Sci. Med. Sci. 67, 652-660.

Brown-Borg, H.M., Borg, K.E., Meliska, C.J., and Bartke, A. (1996). Dwarf mice and the ageing process. Nature 384, 33.

Campbell, T. C. et al. China: from diseases of poverty to diseases of affluence. Policy implications of the epidemiological transition. Ecol. Food Nutr. 27, 133-144 (1992).

Campbell, T. C. & Campbell, T. M., II. The China Study, Startling Implications for Diet, Weight Loss, and Long-Term Health. (BenBella Books, Inc., 2005).

Cappola, A.R., Xue, Q.L., Ferrucci, L., Guralnik, J.M., Volpato, S., and Fried, L.P. (2003). Insulin-like growth factor I and interleukin-6 contribute synergistically to disability and mortality in older women. J. Clin. Endocrinol. Metab. 88, 2019-2025.

Carroll, K. K., Braden, L. M., Bell, J. A. & Kalamegham, R. Fat and cancer. Cancer 58, 1818-1825 (1986).

Carroll, K. K. in Animal and Vegetable Proteins in Lipid Metabolism and Atherosclerosis (eds M.J. Gibney & D. Kritchevsky) 9-17 (Alan R. Liss, Inc., 1983).

Carroll, K. K. & Huff, M. W. in Nutrition and food science, present knowledge and utilization Vol. 3, Nutritional biochemistry and pathology (eds W. Santos, N. Lopes, J.J. Barbosa, & D. Chaves) 379-385 (Plenum Press, 1980).

Cava, E., and Fontana, L. (2013). Will calorie restriction work in humans? Aging (Albany, N.Y. Online) 5, 507-514.

Chen, T.S., Currier, G.J., and Wabner, C.L. (1990). Intestinal transport during the life span of the mouse. J. Gerontol. 45, B129-B133.

Colman, R.J., Anderson, R.M., Johnson, S.C., Kastman, E.K., Kosmatka, K.J., Beasley, T.M., Allison, D.B., Cruzen, C., Simmons, H.A., Kemnitz, J.W., and

Weindruch, R. (2009). Caloric restriction delays disease onset and mortality in rhesus monkeys. Science 325, 201-204.

Conway, J.M., Ingwersen, L.A., and Moshfegh, A.J. (2004). Accuracy of dietary recall using the USDA five-step multiple-pass method in men: an observational validation study. J. Am. Diet. Assoc. 104, 595-603.

Coulston, A.M., and Boushey, C. (2008). Nutrition in the prevention and treatment of disease. (Amsterdam, Boston: Academic Press).

DHHS (2001). U.S. Department of Health and Human Services (DHHS). National Center for Health Statistics. Third National Health and Nutrition Examination Survey, 1988-1994, NJANES III. (Hyattsville, MD: Centers for Disease Control and Prevention).

Esselstyn, C. B., Ellis, S. G., Medendorp, S. V. & Crowe, T. D. A strategy to arrest and reverse coronary artery disease: a 5-year longitudinal study of a single physician's practice. J. Family Practice 41, 560-568 (1995).

Estruch, R., Ros, E., Salas-Salvado, J., Covas, M.I., Corella, D., Aros, F., Gomez-Gracia, E., Ruiz-Gutierrez, V., Fiol, M., Lapetra, J., et al.; PREDIMED Study Investigators (2013). Primary prevention of cardiovascular disease with a Mediterranean diet. N. Engl. J. Med. 368, 1279-1290.

Expert Panel. Food, nutrition and the prevention of cancer, a global perspective. (American Institute for Cancer Research/World Cancer Research Fund, 1997).

Fabrizio, P., Pozza, F., Pletcher, S.D., Gendron, C.M., and Longo, V.D. (2001). Regulation of longevity and stress resistance by Sch9 in yeast. Science 292, 288-290.

Ferrucci, L., Guralnik, J.M., Cavazzini, C., Bandinelli, S., Lauretani, F., Bartali, B., Repetto, L., and Longo, D.L. (2003). The frailty syndrome: a critical issue in geriatric oncology. Crit. Rev. Oncol. Hematol. 46, 127-137.

Flynn, M.A., Nolph, G.B., Baker, A.S., and Krause, G. (1992). Aging in humans: a continuous 20-year study of physiologic and dietary parameters. J. Am. Coll. Nutr. 11, 660-672.

Fontana, L., and Klein, S. (2007). Aging, adiposity, and calorie restriction. JAMA 297, 986-994.

Fontana, L., Klein, S., and Holloszy, J.O. (2006). Long-term low-protein, low-calorie diet and endurance exercise modulate metabolic factors associated with cancer risk. Am. J. Clin. Nutr. 84, 1456-1462.

Fontana, L., Weiss, E.P., Villareal, D.T., Klein, S. and Holloszy, J.O. (2008). Long-term effects of calorie or protein restriction on serum IGF-1 and IGFBP-3 concentration in humans. Aging Cell 7, 681-687.

Fontana, L., Partridge, L., and Longo, V.D. (2010). Extending healthy life span-from yeast to humans. Science 328, 321-326.

Fontana, L., Vinciguerra, M. and Longo, V.D. (2012). Growth factors, nutrient signaling, and cardiovascular aging. Circ. Res. 110, 1139-1150.

Fontana, L., Adelaiye, R.M., Rastelli, A.L., Miles, K.M., Ciamporcero, E., Longo, V.D., Nguyen, H., Vessella, R., and Pili, R. (2013). Dietary protein restriction inhibits tumor growth in human xenograft models. Oncotarget 4, 2451-2461.

Fulgoni, V.L, 3rd. (2008). Current protein intake in America: analysis of the National Health and Nutrition Examination Survey, 2003-2004. Am. J. Clin. Nutr. 87, 1554S-1557S.

Fung, T.T., van Dam, R.M., Hankinson, S.E., Stampfer, M., Willett, W.C., and Hu, F.B. (2010). Low-carbohydrate diets and all-cause and cause-specific mortality: two cohort studies. Ann. Intern. Med. 153, 289-298.

Gallinetti, J.M Harputlugil, E., and Mitchell, J.R. (2013). Amino acid sensing in dietary-restriction-mediated longevity: roles of signal-transducing kinases GCN2 and TOR. Biochem. J. 449, 1-10.

Garry, P.J., Rhyne, R.L., Halioua, L., and Nicholson, C. (1989). Changes in dietary patterns over a 6-year period in an elderly population. Ann. N Y Acad. Sci. 561, 104-112.

Giovannucci, E., Pollak, M., Liu, Y., Platz, E.A., Majeed, N., Rimm, E.B., and Willett, W.C. (2003). Nutritional predictors of insulin-like growth factor I and their relationships to cancer in men. Cancer Epidemiol. Biomarkers Prev. 12, 84-89.

Guarente, L., and Kenyon, C. (2000). Genetic pathways that regulate ageing in model organisms. Nature 408, 255-262.

Hegsted, D. M. Calcium and osteoporosis. J. Nutr. 116, 2316-2319 (1986).

Keys, A. Coronary heart disease in seven countries. Circulation Suppl. 41, I1-I211 (1970).

Keys, A. Seven countries. A multivariate analysis of death and coronary heart disease. (Harvard University Press, 1980).

Kritchevsky, D., Tepper, S. A., Czarnecki, S. K., Klurfeld, D. M. & Story, J. A. in Current Topics in Nutrition and Disease, Volume 8: Animal and Vegetable Proteins in Lipid Metabolism and Atherosclerosis (eds D Kritchevsky & M.J. Gibney) 85-100 (Alan R. Liss, Inc., 1983).

Kritchevsky, D., Tepper, S. A., Czarnecki, S. K. & Klurfeld, D. M. Atherogenicity of animal and vegetable protein. Influence of the lysine to arginine ratio. Atherosclerosis 41, 429-431 (1982).

Larsson, S. C. & Orsini, N. Red meat and processed meat consumption and all-cause mortality: a meta-analysis. Am. J. Epidemiol. 179, 282-289 (2013).

Madhavan, T. V. & Gopalan, C. The effect of dietary protein on carcinogenesis of aflatoxin. Arch. Path. 85, 133-137 (1968).

Meeker, D. R. & Kesten, H. D. Experimental atherosclerosis and high protein diets. Proc. Soc. Exp. Biol. Med. 45, 543-545 (1940).

Meeker, D. R. & Kesten, H. D. Effect of high protein diets on experimental atherosclerosis of rabbits. Arch. Pathology 31, 147-162 (1941).

Newburgh, L. H. & Clarkson, S. Production of atherosclerosis in rabbits by diet rich in animal protein. JAMA 79, 1106-1108 (1922).

Newburgh, L. H. & Clarkson, S. The production of arteriosclerosis in rabbits by feeding diets rich in meat. Arch. Intern. Med. 31, 653-676 (1923).

Schulsinger, D. A., Root, M. M. & Campbell, T. C. Effect of dietary protein quality on development of aflatoxin B1-induced hepatic preneoplastic lesions. J. Natl. Cancer Inst. 81, 1241-1245 (1989).

Sirtori, C. R., Agradi, E., Conti, F., Mantero, O. & Gatti, E. Soybean-protein diet in the treatment of type II hyperlipoproteinemia. Lancet 1(8006), 275-277 (1977).

Terpstra, A. H. M., Hermus, R. J. J. & West, C. E. in Animal and Vegetable Proteins in Lipid Metabolism and Athersclerosis (eds M.J. Gibney & D. Kritchevsky) 19-49 (Alan R. Liss, Inc., 1983).

Wallace, J.I., Schwartz, R.S., LaCroix, A.Z., Uhlmann, R.F., and Pearlman, R.A. (1995). Involuntary weight loss in older outpatients: incidence and clinical significance. J. Am. Geriatr. Soc. 43, 329-337.

Wei, M., Fabrizio, P., Hu, J., Ge, H., Cheng, C., Li, L., and Longo, V.D. (2008). Life span extension by calorie restriction depends on Rim15 and transcription factors downstream of Ras/PKA, Tor, and Sch9. PLoS Genet. 4, e13.

Wei, M., Fabrizio, P., Madia, F., Hu, J., Ge, H., Li, L.M., and Longo, V.D. (2009). Tor1/Sch9-regulated carbon source substitution is as effective as calorie restriction in life span extension. PLoS Genet. 5, e10000467.

Willett, W.C. (2006). The Mediterranean diet: science and practice. Public Health Nutr. 9 (1A), 105-110.

Wolpin, B.M., Michaud, D.S., Giovannucci, E.L., Schernhammer, E.S., Stampfer, M.J., Manson, J.E., Cochrane, B.B., Rohan, T.E., Ma, J., Pollak, M.N., and Fuchs,

C.S. (2007). Circulating insulin-like growth factor binding protein-1 and the risk of pancreatic cancer. Cancer Res. 67, 7923-7928.

Woudstra, T., and Thomson, A.B. (2002). Nutrient absorption and intestinal adaptation with ageing. Best Pract. Res. Clin. Gastroenterol. 16, 1-15.

Youngman, L.D. (1993). Protein restriction (PR) and caloric restriction (CR) compared: effects on DNA damage, carcinogenesis, and oxidative damage. Mutat. Res. 295, 165-179.

CHAPTER 3
RICE PROTEIN

INTRODUCTION

Rice protein is derived from whole rice grain that has had variable portions of its outer layer removed during processing. This means that many forms of commercially available rice protein powders still contain fiber to a varying degree. Rice protein is available in concentrates or isolates. Enzymatic treatment of brown rice separates its protein and carbohydrate contents resulting in protein fractions that are a significant source of branched chain amino acids (BCAA), such as leucine and isoleucine. These BCAA assist in stimulating protein synthesis and reducing the catabolic breakdown of protein. However, rice protein is low in its content of lysine, but it has a valuable content of sulfur containing amino acids (cysteine and methionine).

An ideal complementary protein that can be used together with rice protein is pea protein. Pea protein is relatively high in lysine but it has modest contents of cysteine and methionine. Most concentrated rice protein is hypoallergenic and it has a significant fiber content (about 10% of mixed soluble and insoluble fiber). Rice protein has a distinctive, less bitter taste than whey or pea protein. The flavor of the rice protein is quite acceptable to many consumers and it may help to avoid needs for pronounced artificial flavoring.

Rice protein processing involves the removal of the outermost layer (the hull) of the whole rice grain to form brown rice. Further milling and processing of rice produces white rice which can be further polished, as required. The conversion process of brown to white rice has a major effect on reducing the nutritional value of rice with a substantial loss of B vitamins, micronutrients (manganese, selenium, phosphorus, and iron), dietary fiber and essential fatty acids. In the U.S. rice that has been completely milled and polished is enriched with vitamins B and iron to improve its nutritional quality.

NUTRITION AND RICE PROTEIN

Many factors determine the nutritional value of various types of rice. Major species of rice include Oryza sativa and Orzyza glaberrima (African rice). Rice is a staple food for about 50% of the world population and supplies about 20% of total dietary energy consumed by humans. Rice protein has a high concentration of premium proteins with an amino acid profile that supports many body structures and functions in active adults. As mentioned, rice protein is a valuable source of branched chain amino acids (BCAA) such as leucine, which is important for muscle recovery and muscle protein synthesis, especially following exercise. While rice protein may have lower digestibility scores than whey, egg, or soy protein, it falls into a category of plentiful bio-availability as defined by the Digestible Indispensable Amino Acid Score (DIAAS). In recent times, measurement of the DIAAS has been considered a preferred method to the PDCAAS (Protein Digestibility Corrected Amino Acid Scores) (Chapter 1).

While the DIAAS method of protein evaluation records higher values of dairy protein compared with plant protein, rice protein is advantageous due to its contents of both arginine and leucine. Arginine is known to be a rate-limiting factor in protein synthesis and it releases many bioactive compounds, such as nitric oxide. In addition, arginine promotes the release of growth hormone in humans. Moreover, arginine is a catalyst for the synthesis of creatine, which is important for muscle performance and maintenance. It is notable that rice protein often has a greater arginine content than proteins acquired from whey, casein, soy, and peas. In brief, the amino acid profile in rice protein permits it to be used as a healthy, multifunctional supplement in a variety of foods and beverages.

RICE PROTEIN HAS A MODEST GLYCEMIC INDEX

Rice protein has a modest glycemic index and is absorbed over an intermediate to a relatively long period following ingestion, in comparison to whey protein, which is a considered to be a "fast protein" (see Chapter 1). As a result, rice protein causes only modest fluctuations in blood sugar (a low glycemic index) and insulin levels. This circumstance helps rice to maintain a consistent source of energy. In experimental animals, rice protein produced by enzymatic methods (RP-E) has a relatively low digestibility score, which is an important contributor to its known cardiovascular health benefits. These benefits of a low digestibility include nutritional support for cholesterol lowering, triglyceride lowering, and assistance in control of body weight.

MUSCLE RECOVERY

Some people believe that fast muscle recovery is produced mainly by whey protein, but there is little evidence that immediate protein responses are necessary or specifically valuable following exercise. Intermediate or slower digestible proteins, as found in rice protein, can exhibit inhibitory effects on whole body protein breakdown, muscle glycogen depletion, fatigue or tiredness, decreased athletic performance and imbalances between carbohydrate and protein metabolism.

FIBER CONTENT

Apart from the health benefits of rice protein, there are clear advantages to its physical and chemical properties that make it ideal for inclusion in a variety of foods and beverages. The presence of a small but definite amount of soluble fiber in certain types of rice protein permits actions similar to gel fibers that improve mouth-feel but and assist in stabilizing protein shakes. Gel fibers reduce the glycemic index of mixed meals largely due to an effect on delaying gastric emptying (Holt S, et al, The Effect of Gel Fiber....., Lancet 1:636-9, 1979).

AMINO ACID PROFILE

There is an anticipated minor variation in the amino acid profile of rice protein that occurs during natural enzymatic manufacturing processes. Rice protein is a complete source of protein that contains a wide array of amino acids as shown in Table 15 below.

Amino Acids	Milligrams per 100g Protein In 80% Rice Protein Isolate	Amino Acids	Milligrams per 100g Protein In 80% Rice Protein Isolate

Aspartic Acid	7,230	Leucine	6,840
Threonine	2,960	Isoleucine	3,610
Serine	4,020	Tyrosine	4,530
Glutamic Acid	14,500	Phenylalanine	4,580
Proline	3,920	Lysine	2,580
Glycine	3,600	Histidine	1,770
Alanine	4,780	Valine	4,720
Arginine	6,780	Tryptophan	1,100
Cystine	1,820	Methionine	2,400

Table 15. An amino acid profile of one commercially available type of rice protein (80% concentrate).

MORE ON THE GLYCEMIC INDEX OF RICE PROTEIN

The glycemic index is essentially a mechanism of blood sugar profiling that can be calculated, measured, or inferred for many different foods. Foods have variable effects on blood glucose profile following ingestion. Research shows that it is possible to define the glycemic index of many foods. The glycemic index is controlled to a significant degree by the rate at which the stomach empties its contents into the small bowel (Holt S. et al, The Effect of Gel Fiber…. Lancet 1:636-9, 1979).

Foods differ in physical and chemical characteristics and factors such as energy density, pH, temperature, and viscosity. These factors can affect the rate at which gastric emptying occurs. For example, the efficiency of chewing food, which affects ingested particle size and the degree of food hydration are factors that can alter the rate of glucose and other nutrient absorption during digestion. Rice provides an example of how the glycemic index of a foodstuff can be varied to a significant degree by the presence of soluble rice fiber (amylose). A high amylose content of rice will produce a higher viscosity effect (gelatinization). This will result in a further lowering of the glycemic index, by delaying absorption of glucose.

Protein generally acts to lower blood sugar levels when it is combined as part of a carbohydrate meal, due to its ability to stimulate insulin secretion. However, the amount of protein required to simulate significant reductions in blood glucose is quite high (of the order of 50 gm or 12 oz. of protein). Rice protein has a special benefit for non-insulin dependent diabetics where slow absorption of carbohydrate from rice protein is combined with a reasonable protein availability.

Another medicinal (nutritional) area in which rice protein may be quite valuable is in menopausal and mature women to induce slower rises in glucose and insulin responses that tend to last over a post-prandial period of 3 to 5 hours, (Gillespie L, The Menopause Diet, Health, Life Publications, pp24, 25, 1999). Rice protein may be an ideal option for the females who want to avoid the phytoestrogen (isoflavone) content of soy protein.

OTHER ADVANTAGES OF RICE PROTEIN

Allergic reactions to rice protein are very uncommon, with isolated reports of occasional eczema and bowel disturbance. There is a clear hierarchy of a tendency to allergy among different sources of protein. The most common food allergens in order of occurrence of allergic reactions are found in: peanuts, soybeans, milk protein (such as casein or whey), eggs, seafood, sesame seeds, tree nuts, and wheat. In brief, rice protein is hypoallergenic and gluten free. Gluten may cause gluten enteropathy (*celiac disease*), which in turn results in malabsorption and variable manifestations of auto- immunity. Gluten enteropathy is due to delayed hypersensitivity reactions and it is distinguished from general wheat protein allergy.

The protein content of rice has been shown to function in aerobic fitness enthusiasts in a similar manner to whey protein (Joy JM et al Nut.J., 2013, 12(1), 86). Marketing platforms and promotions of whey protein have tended to focus on the superiority of whey protein in increasing muscle mass, with the inaccurate conclusion that vegetable protein is not as effective as whey protein for muscle building in athletes.

Recent studies of the effects of 8 weeks of whey or rice protein supplementation on body composition and exercise performance show that both whey and rice protein isolate have substantial equivalence in overall outcome (Jaeger R. Nat. Prod. Expo, March 9, 2013). Both whey and rice protein isolate administration, following resistance exercise, improves indices of body composition and exercise performance. In these comparative studies of whey and rice protein, there were no detectable differences in psychometric scores of perceived recovery, body soreness, or readiness to train. Moreover, other positive effects were observed in which lean body mass, muscle mass, strength, and power all increased, while fat mass decreased (Jaeger, ibid, 2013).

There are several other reported benefits of rice protein which include a reduction of oxidative stress as a result of its contents of free radical scavengers (antioxidants). In addition, there may be significant boosting of immune function, which can be attenuated sometimes by heavy exercise. The promotion of cardiovascular health is a very important and pivotal advantage of rice protein consumption. Rice protein can also contribute to effective weight control and post exercise muscle recovery. These qualities of rice protein tend to dismiss the old fashioned notion that fast protein absorption is necessarily better (e.g. whey administration). There is a growing interest in what has been termed the "slow protein" movement.

Of great significance is the versatile and neutral taste and pleasant smell of rice protein isolate. This makes it an acceptable ingredient in protein powders, shakes, nutrition bars, or as a component for desserts, baked goods, and confectionary.

RICE PROTEIN AND CARDIOVASCULAR HEALTH

Rice protein and rice bran are identified as important nutritional components of a heart healthy lifestyle (USA Rice Federation, February 2, 2011). The U.S. Food and Drug Administration concur with this opinion and diets rich in whole grain and other cereal proteins, such as rice protein, have a low or absent fat content and do not contain cholesterol. This can help reduce the chances of heart disease and some types of cancer. Rice that is not over processed still contains vitamins of the B series and folic acid, which are known to be protective against fatal coronary heart disease and stroke risk. That said, highly processed commercially available rice often contains added B vitamins and iron.

Many individuals who consume enriched white rice or whole grain brown rice have what is generally considered to be a well-balanced diet that assists in the prevention of chronic disease (www.usarice.com). Rice protein contains healthy amounts of complex carbohydrates and dietary fiber, with its approximate 10% fiber content.

RICE PROTEIN MAY LOWER BLOOD PRESSURE

As noted previously, rice protein offers a pleasant tasting food source and it can provide a nutritious base for many rice recipes that can promote cardiovascular structure and function. In addition to supporting healthy blood cholesterol and triglyceride levels, rice protein has a recognized role in supporting a healthy blood pressure level. The widely acclaimed DASH (Dietary Approaches to Stop Hypertension) studies that were proposed by the National Institutes of Health, suggest that eating 6 to 8 servings per day of whole grains will help to control blood pressure.

One potential mechanism of this effect of rice protein on blood pressure relates to the presence of Angiotensin-Converting-Enzyme (ACE)-Inhibitor compounds which may lower blood pressure (vide-infra). Also, rice protein is low in sodium. Based on experimental studies in animals and observations in humans, rice protein can provide nutritional support to promote a healthy blood cholesterol, triglycerides, and blood pressure.

RICE PROTEIN LOWERS BLOOD CHOLESTEROL

While many people have claimed the advantages of high digestibility of certain proteins such as whey, it appears that the lower protein digestibility of rice protein can be a factor contributing to the ability of this protein source to lower blood cholesterol. What has often and inadvertently been perceived to be an advantage of some protein products, such as the ability of whey protein, to increase protein digestibility, can actually be a disadvantage that results in increasing cholesterol absorption and altering lipid profiles (Yang Lin, Int.J.Med. Sci., 2011, 12 (11): 7594-7608).

There is a residual lack of observations on the effect of rice protein on human cholesterol metabolism in Western medical literature. The pivotal studies by Yang Lin et al (ibid) were performed in rats, but there is a prevailing opinion that the ability of rats and humans to digest protein is similar (Gilani et al J. of AOAC International, May 1, 2005). In the studies performed by Lin et al (ibid, 2011), the experimental animals were placed on a cholesterol free diet and the effects of alkali extracted rice proteins (RP-A) and amylase (enzyme) extracted rice proteins

(RP-E) were studied in relation to effects on cholesterol metabolism. In these studies, both the in vivo and in vitro digestibility of RP-A and RP-E were found to be significantly lower than casein (CAS).

Significant lowering of cholesterol levels was observed in rats fed RP-A and RP-E, with lower protein digestibility in rats fed with RP-A versus RP-E. Cholesterol absorption was inhibited more in RP-E treated group versus the RP-A treated animals. This effect was related to the finding of more neutral steroids excreted in the bile of rats that were fed RP-E.

In these latter studies, correlations were noted between protein digestibility and blood cholesterol levels. This study shows the benefit of lower digestibility of rice protein extracted by alkaline or enzymatic processing (RP-A and RP-E, respectively) on cholesterol metabolism. Yang Lin et al (ibid) concluded that the digestibility of rice protein is a major factor in influencing cholesterol metabolism.

LIPID AND GLUCOSE HOMEOSTASIS WITH RICE PROTEIN

In an article by Ronis MJ et al (Exp. Biol. Med, Sept. 2010, 235, 9, 1102-13), rice protein isolates were shown to improve lipid and glucose homeostasis in rats who were fed high fat/high cholesterol diets. In these studies, peroxisome proliferator-activated (PPAR) genes and proteins involved in fatty acid degradation were found to be upregulated by feeding rice protein isolates (RPI).

Similar effects of RPI on hepatic PPAR were also detected and RPI also increased hepatic genes involved in cholesterol metabolism and transport. Overall, increased liver triglyceride content, high blood cholesterol, and insulin resistance were partially prevented by feeding RPI. Messenger ribonucleic acid (MRNA) and protein expression of liver enzymes involved in fatty acid synthesis were suppressed by feeding RPI in the rats who were receiving a high fat/high cholesterol diet.

Ronis et al (ibid, 2010) concluded that the observed attenuation of "metabolic syndrome" in the experimental animals, which occurred in the RPI fed rats on high fat/high cholesterol diets, results from PPAR activation. By inference, these data suggest that in humans, rice protein may be valuable in the management of metabolic Syndrome X which affects approximately 83 million Americans (according to recent CDC statistics).

Additional research confirms the beneficial effects of rice protein on lipid metabolism. Tong X et al (Lipids in Health and Disease, 2012, 11, 1, 24-42) studied the effect of RP-A (alkaline extracted protein) versus RP-E (alpha amylase extracted protein) on triglyceride metabolism in rats fed cholesterol – enriched diets for 2 weeks, as compared with casein (CAS). The feeding of RP (RP-A and RE-E) resulted in significantly lower plasma concentrations of glucose and lipids. In addition, less hepatic accumulation of lipids was apparent as a consequence of RP-feeding.

In these experiments, the administration of RP also depressed hepatic activities of fatty acid synthase (FAS), glucose 6-phosphate dehydrogenase (G6PD), and malate dehydrogenase (MDH). In contrast, activities of lipoprotein lipase (PL) and hepatic lipase were stimulated to a significant degree, compared with CAS feeding (casein). There was a significant positive correlation coefficient demonstrated between protein digestibility and body fat deposition and a similar correlation between protein digestibility and plasma triglyceride (TG) concentrations. These data support the notion that lower digestibility of rice protein is a real advantage in controlling blood lipids compared with other sources of protein, such as whey protein.

The authors of the study Tong X et al (ibid, 2012) concluded that: *"the present study demonstrates that rice protein can modify triglyceride metabolism, leading to an improvement of body weight and adiposity. Results suggest that the triglyceride – lowering action as well as the potential of anti-adiposity induced by rice protein is attributed to upregulation of lipolysis and downregulation of lipogenesis, and the lower digestibility of rice protein may be the main modulator responsible for the lipid-lowering action"* (Tong X, et al, ibid, 202).

Rice protein hydrolysates contain variable amounts of blood pressure lowering substances called Angiotensin 1 – Converting-Enzyme (ACE)-Inhibitors. Angiotensin 1 – Converting-Enzyme (ACE) converts angiotensin I to angiotensin II, which has vasopressor (blood pressure elevating) actions. In addition, ACE inhibitors can inactivate bradykinin and regulate local levels of other active peptides (e.g. enkephalins and substance P), which may further result in the lowering of blood pressure.

ACE inhibitors are abundant in rice dregs, which are byproducts of fermentation or other water processing techniques of rice. While many food proteins contain ACE inhibitors, rice dregs are a particularly rich source of vasoactive peptides and they are relatively high in protein content. Other sources of variable amounts of ACE inhibitors are gelatin, maize, whey, fish, and egg protein but these compounds are not as prominent as the levels of ACE inhibitors found in rice dregs (Guo-ging He et al, Journal of Zheijan University, Sci B, June 6(6) 508-513, 2005, English translation).

Many peptides are derived from food protein hydrolysis processes and it would be expected that ACE inhibitors are bio-available as a consequence of rice protein consumption. Chinese researchers have demonstrated the antihypertensive effect of rice protein hydrolysate in spontaneously hypertensive laboratory animals and discovered an ACE inhibitor peptide with the amino acid sequence Thr-Gln-Val-Tyr (Guan-Hong Li et al Asia Pac. J. Clin. Nutr. 2007, 16 (Suppl1) 275-280). In animal studies performed at the National Research Institute in Japan, rice bran was found to lower blood pressure with a degree of activity similar to ACE inhibitor drugs.

In summary, there are many favorable properties of rice protein (Table 16)

- Hypoallergenic
- Good protein digestibility
- Antioxidative performance
- Moisture management
- Gluten free
- Thermo-stable
- Fast and high dispersibility
- Competitive-cost protein
- pH stable
- Long shelf life

- Protein-interaction synergism
- Reduces surface tension at water: fat interface
- Neutral taste and flavor profile
- Rich tan color
- Low to zero environmental footprint
- Ecologically sustainable
- Salt-tolerant
- Reasonable solubility
- Label-friendly and consumer awareness
- Most essential amino acids for growth and function

Table 16 Adapted from Hoogenkamp H, Rice Protein and Beyond, ISBN-13, 1490396620, 2013.

INCREASING POPULARITY OF RICE PROTEIN

Compared with whey and soy protein there has been a recent meteoric rise in the use of rice protein for its valuable role in healthy fitness plans. This interest is fueled by the benefits of rice protein for cardiovascular health, its absence of lactose and gluten and its fiber content. While whey protein has been considered to be a premium standard with its high protein content and desirable essential amino acid profile, more protein is not necessarily better, when considering the health benefits of various protein sources (American Diabetes Association Guidelines). To reiterate important concepts addressed earlier, the lower digestibility score of rice protein appears to be valuable for health.

It is unusual for people in developed countries not to eat a reasonably balanced diet that complements daily needs of essential amino acids. Some scientists believe that the value of whey protein has been "hyped" at the expense of considering the drawbacks of its contents of lactose, cholesterol, milk protein, limited gastrointestinal tolerance and its allergenic potential. Moreover, rice protein often has a residual and valuable vitamin and mineral contents. Rice protein is less likely to produce hyperaminoacidemia than whey protein and this may have the theoretical advantage of lowering renal and hepatic stress during extra protein consumption.

CONTAMINANTS IN RICE

Rice may be contaminated with several substances. Of most concern is contamination with arsenic. Researchers at the University of Aberdeen in Scotland (U.K.) have reported that rice grown in the U.S. has 1.4 to 5 times more arsenic content than rice from Europe, India, or Bangladesh. There is no "safe" level of arsenic which is highly toxic element in many organ systems in humans. Arsenic is classified as a group 1 cancer causing agent- (carcinogen).

Studies of rice contamination with arsenic have revealed some conflicting results, but rice from India and Thailand appear to be the least contaminated with arsenic (Potera, C., Food Safety: U.S. Rice Serves Up Arsenic, Environmental Health Perspectives, 115, 6, 2007). While U.S. rice tends to contain the highest levels of arsenic, the more toxic inorganic form of arsenic tend to be found in greater amounts in rice cultivated in India, Bangladesh, and Europe.

The presence of arsenic in U.S. rice seems to be linked to earlier use of land for cotton growing (especially in the states of Mississippi and Arkansas). Cotton crops in certain locations were often treated with arsenic containing pesticides. In fact, when rice farms were first developed in cotton growing areas in the U.S., arsenic-related disease was encountered in individuals who consumed contaminated rice as a dietary staple.

This circumstance has led to preferences for organic rice from countries with lower arsenic presence, e.g. Thailand and adjacent countries. Evidence of the degree of vigilance over soil testing for arsenic and other toxic contaminants is quite variable in certain locations. A limit of 150 parts per billion is the upper limit of arsenic in rice in China, but guidelines are not clarified in the U.S., except for an upper limit of arsenic in drinking water of 10 ppb that was proposed in 2012. Recently, there has been a focus on the presence of tungsten in brown rice products. Tungsten is a metal with high tensile strength that may cause acute and chronic toxicity. It is a carcinogen in long term studies.

The presence of heavy metals in rice protein presents a public health concern, which has led to an industry agreement among several suppliers to agree to limit heavy metal contamination of protein products (www.naturalnews.com/043792-rice-protein-heavy-metals-industry-agreement.html). The new agreement sets the following limits for heavy metals in protein products to be: lead 250 ppb, tungsten 50 ppb, cadmium 1,000 ppb, and mercury 50 ppb. (These are suggested limits of heavy metals in rice protein that have not been set with clarity by regulatory agencies, at the time of writing).

A further potential contaminant of rice and rice protein is cadmium, which enters the rice plant via industrial waste or sometimes via certain types of fertilizer. Cadmium has been associated with renal toxicity with loss of glucose and amino acids in the urine (nephrotoxicity).

PROBLEMS WITH RICE PROTEIN SUPPLEMENTS

Rice protein has gained a reputation for being the safest of the available protein supplements. Rice protein is best produced by enzymatic removal of its starch content and treatment with alkaline solutions. This process is free of damaging or toxic chemicals, in contrast with other protein processing which may involve organic chemical treatments (e.g. soy or hexane-extracted rice protein).

Rice protein has a very low tendency to cause allergies. It is regarded as hypoallergenic. There are unsubstantiated reports in the Orient of some cases of rice allergy associated with eczema and enterocolitis has been described in Croatia following rice protein use. In this latter case, it is not clear if the rice protein was contaminated by other proteins or allergens.

Much has been discussed about the composition of rice protein in terms of its amino acid content. It is clear that rice protein contains most essential and non-essential amino acids, but low levels of certain amino acids are encountered in rice e.g. methionine, cysteine and lysine. This has led to the recognition that other dietary protein additions to rice protein are necessary to produce a "complete" protein intake.

SUMMING-UP ON RICE PROTEIN

In summary, the main characteristics of rice protein include the following:

- **High Protein Concentration.** Rice protein can be concentrated (up to about 80%), to act as an efficient source of many essential amino acids.
- **Rice Protein has low or absent allergy potential.** In contrast to whey and egg protein, allergic reactions to rice protein have been reported to be very uncommon.
- **Rice Protein Has a Reduced Glycemic Index.** Rapid spikes in blood glucose (a high glycemic index) can cause insulin resistance to occur over time. Unlike plain white rice the glycemic index of rice protein is beneficially modest.

- **Rice Protein is Gluten Free.** Wheat protein is a source of gluten that can cause damage to the small intestinal lining (celiac disease), in susceptible individuals.
- **Nutritional Support for a Healthy Blood Pressure.** Rice protein is regarded as heart healthy and is low in sodium. Angiotensin-1-converting enzyme (ACE) creates angiotensin II, which raises blood pressure. Rice protein contains variable amounts of ACE inhibitors that may act to support a healthy blood pressure by blocking this enzymatic conversion.
- **Rice Protein is Cholesterol Free.** Rice protein is free of cholesterol and is known to promote a lower blood cholesterol and triglycerides in experimental circumstances, especially when it is processed with an enzymatic method or in an alkaline environment.
- **Rice Protein is Lactose Free.** Lactose is a sugar that may present digestive problems in individuals with a deficiency of the enzyme lactase that causes lactose intolerance. Whey protein contains lactose, but rice protein is lactose free. Whey may also cause significant digestive upset, independent of its lactose content.
- **Rice Protein has High Fiber Content.** Rice protein has 10% of mixed bioactive insoluble and soluble fiber, in contrast to many other protein supplements.
- **Benefits During Exercise Equivalent to Whey Protein.** Recent studies document the ability of rice protein supplementation to function as effectively as equivalent amounts of whey protein, with comparable benefits on lean body mass, muscle hypertrophy, and power and strength following resistance exercises (Jaeger R Nat. Prod. Expo, March 9, 2013).

RICE PROTEIN REFERENCES

Anderson, A.K. and H.S. Guraya, 2001. Extractability of protein in physically processed rice bran. J. Am. Oil Chem. Soc., 78: 969-972.

Arai T, Takaya T, Ito Y, Hayakawa K, Toshima S, Shibuya C, et al. Bronchial asthma induced by rice. Intern Med. 1998;37:98–101.

Ayano Y., F. Ohta, Y. Watanabe, and K. Mita. 1980. Dietary fiber fractions in defatted rice bran and their hypocholesterolernic effect in cholesterol-fed rats.

B. O. Eggum, B. O. Juliano, and C. C. Magningat, 1982, Protein and energy utilization of rice milling fractions, Journal of Human Nutrition, 31, 371 – 376.

Bean, M.M. and K.D. Nishita. 1985. Rice flours for baking. In: Rice Chemistry and Technology. (Ed.): B.O. Juliano. AACC International, St. Paul, MN, pp. 539-556.

Bera, M.B. and R.K. Mukherjee, 1988. Nutritional evaluation of rice bran protein concentrate. Ind. J. Nutr. Diet., 25: 50-54.

Bhattacharjee, P., Singhal, R.S. & Kulkarni, P.R. (2002). Basmati rice: a review. International Journal of Food Science and Technology, 37, 1–12.

Brand-Miller J., Hayne S., Petocz P., Colagiuri S. Low–glycemic index diets in the management of diabetes: A meta-analysis of randomized controlled trials. Diabetes Care. 2003;26:2261–2267.

C. S. James, 1995, Mineral elements in rice, Analytical Chemistry of Food, Blackle Academic and Professional Publishers, New York, 126 – 128.

Cagampang, G., L. Cruz, S. Espiritu, R. Santiago and B.O. Juliano. 1966. Studies on the extraction and composition of rice proteins. Cereal Chem., 43: 145-155.

Chandi, G.K. and D.S. Sogi, 2007. Functional properties of rice bran protein concentrates J. Food Eng. 79:592-597.

Chavan, J. and S. Duggal. 1978. Studies on the essential amino acid composition, protein fractions and biological value (BV) of some new varieties of rice. J. Sci. Food Agri., 29: 225-229.

Chen Z.Y., Jiao R., Ma K.Y. Cholesterol-lowering nutraceuticals and functional foods. J. Agric. Food Chem. 2008;56:8761–8773.

Choudhury, N.H. & Juliano, B.O. (1980a). Lipids in developing and mature rice grain. Phytochemistry, 19, 1063–1069.

Chrastil, J. 1992. Correlations between the physicochemical and functional properties of rice. J. Agri. Food Chem., 40:1683-1686.

Del Rosario, A.R., Briones, V.P., Vidal, A.J. & Juliano, B.O. (1968). Composition and endosperm structure of developing and mature rice kernel. Cereal Chemistry, 45, 225–235.

First Double Blind Study Proves Plant-based Rice Protein has Identical Benefits to Animal-based Whey Protein (News article/1349955/First-Double-Blind-Study-Proves-Plant-based-Rice-Protein-Has-Identical-Benefits).

Garlick PJ: The role of leucine in the regulation of protein metabolism. J Nutr 2005, 135:1553S-1556S.

Gerhardt A. L., and N. B. Gallo. 1998. Full-fat rice bran and oat bran similarly reduce hyper-cholesterolernia in humans. J. Nutc 128:865-869.

Hargrove, K.L.Jr., 1994. Processing and utilization of rice bran in the United States. In: W. E. Marshall and J. I. Wadsworth (Eds.), Rice science and technology. New York: Marcel Dekker Inc., pp: 381-404.

Haumann, B. F. 1989. Rice bran linked to lower cholesterol. J. Am. Oil Chemists Soc. 66:615-618.

Health Benefits of Rice Bran: a Review. J. Nutr.Food Sci. 2011. 1:3. Nagendra Prasad.

Hegsted M., M.M. Windhauser, S. K. Morris, and S. B. Lester. 1993. Stabilized rice bran and oat bran lower cholesterol in humans. Nutr. Res. 13:387-398.

Hemavathy, J. & Prabhakar, J.V. (1987). Lipid composition of rice (Oryza sativa L.) bran. Journal of the American Oil Chemists' Society, 64, 1016–1019.

Hoogenkamp, Henk. Rice Bran Isolate: The alternative for soy protein? Poultry Processing, April 2008, 20-22.

Houston, D.F. (1967). High protein flour can be made from all types of milled rice. Rice Journal, 70, 12–15.

Isono, H., Ohtsubo, K., Iwasaki, T. & Yamazaki, A. (1994). Eating quality of domestic and foreign rices of various varieties and characteristics. Journal of the Japanese Society for Food Science and Technology-Nippon Shokuhin Kogyo Gakkaishi, 41, 485–492.

Jenkins D.J.A., Kendall C.W.C., Augustin L.S.A., Franceschi S., Hamidi M., Marchie A., Jenkins A.L., Axelsen M. Glycemic index: Overview of implications in health and disease. Am. J. Clin. Nutr. 2002;76:266S–273S.

Juliano, B.O. (1985a). Production and utilization of rice. In: Rice Chemistry and Technology (edited by B.O. Juliano). Pp. 1–16. St Paul, Minnesota: American Association of Cereal Chemists.

Juliano, B.O. 1985. Polysaccharides, proteins, and lipids. In: Rice: chemistry and technology. (Ed.): B.O. Juliano. AACC, St. Paul, pp. 59-174.

Khush G. Productivity improvements in rice. Nutr Rev. 2003;61:S114–116. doi: 01301/nr.2003.jun.S114-S116.

Kumagai T., Kawamura H., Fuse T., Watanabe T., Sato Y., Masumura T., Watanabe R., Kadowaki M. Production of rice protein by alkaline extraction improves its digestibility. J. Nutr. Sci. Vitaminol. 2006;52:467–472.

Levin B.E., Hogan S., Sullivan A.C. Initiation and perpetuation of obesity and obesity resistance in rats. Am. J. Physiol. 1989; 256:R766–R771.

Ludwig D.S., Majzoub J.A., Al-Zahrani A., Dallal G.E., Blanco I., Roberts S.B. High glycemic index foods, overeating, and obesity. Pediatrics. 1999;103 doi: 10.1542/peds.103.3.e26.

Lumdubwong, N. & Seib, P.A. (2000). Rice starch isolation by alkaline protease digestion of wet-milled rice flour. Journal of Cereal Science, 31, 63–74.

Malinow, M. R., P. McLaugwin, L. Papworth, H. K. Naito, and L. A. Lewis. 1976. Effect of bran and cholestyramine on plasma lipids in monkeys. Am. J. Clin. Nutr, 29:905-911.

Miller J.B., Pang E., Bramall L. Rice: A high or low glycemic index food? Am. J. Clin. Nutr. 1992;56:1034–1036.

Morita T., Oh-hashi A., Takei K., Ikai M., Kasaoka S., Kiryama S. Cholesterol-lowering effects of soybean, potato and rice proteins depend on their low methionine contents in rats fed a cholesterol-free purified diet. J. Nutr. 1997; 127:470–477.

Normand, F.L., Soignet, D.M., Hogan, J.T. & Deobald,H.J. (1966). Content of certain nutrients and amino acid patterns in high-protein rice flour. Rice Journal, 69, 13–18.

Padhye, V.W. & Salunkhe, D.K. (1979). Extraction and characterization of rice protein. Cereal Chemistry, 56, 389–393.

Panlasigui L.N., Thompson L.U. Blood glucose lowering effects of brown rice in normal and diabetic subjects. Int. J. Food Sci. Nutr. 2006;57:151–158.

Prakash, J., 1996. Rice bran proteins: Properties and food uses. Crit. Rev. Food Sci. Nutr., 36: 537-552.

Sanders, T. A. B., and S. Reddy. 1992. The influence of rice bran on plasma lipids and lipoproteins in human volunteers Eu,-. I. Cl/n. Nut r. 46:167-172.

Shibasaki M, Suzuki S, Nemoto H, Kuroume T. Allergenicity and lymphocyte-stimulating property of rice protein. J Allergy Clin Immunol. 1979; 64:259–265. doi: 10.1016/0091-6749(79)90141-6.

Shih, F. 2004. Rice proteins. In: Rice Chemistry and Technology. (Ed.): E.T. Champagne. AACC International, St. Paul, MN. pp. 143-157.

Sun Q., Donna S., Rob M.V.D., Michelle D.H., Vasanti S.M., Walter C.W., Frank B.H. White rice, brown rice, and risk of type 2 diabetes in US men and women. Arch. Intern. Med. 2010;170:961–969.

Suzanne D, Donald KL: Protein metabolic roles in treatment of obesity. Curr Opin Clin Nutr Metab Care 2010, 13:403-407.

Tanaka, K., Sugimoto, T., Ogawa, M. & Kasai, Z. (1980). Isolation and characterization of two types of protein bodies in the rice endosperm. Agricultural and Biological Chemistry, 44, 1633–1639.

Tanaka, K., T. Sugimoto, M. Ogawa and Z. Kasai. 1980. Isolation and characterization of two types of protein bodies in the rice endosperm. Agri. Biol. Chem., 44: 1633-1639.

Trowell, H. C. 1975. Refined Foods and Disease, Burkitt and Trowell, Eds., Academic Press, London, 195-226.

USA Rice Federation, 2002, The natural history of rice, Food and Cultural Encyclopedia, 1-4.

Yang L, Chen JH, Xu T, Qiu W, Zhang Y, Zhang LW, Xu FP, Liu HB. Rice protein extracted by different methods affects cholesterol metabolism in rats due to its lower digestibility. Int J Mol Sci. 2011;12:7594–7608. doi: 10.3390/ijms12117594.

Yoshino, G., T. Kazumj, M. Amano, M. Tateiwa, T. Yamasakim, S. Takashima, M. Iwai, H. Hatanaka, and S. Baba. 1989. Effects of gamma-oryzanol and probucol on hyperlipidemia. Current Therap. Res. 45:975-982.

Zhang G., Malik V.S., Pan A., Kumar S., Holmes M.D., Spiegelman D., Lin X., Hu F.B. Substituting brown rice for white rice to lower diabetes risk: A focus-group study in Chinese adults. J. Am. Diet. Assoc. 2010; 110:1216–1221.

Zhang H, Bartley GE, Mitchell CR, Zhang H, Yokoyama W: Lower weight gain and hepatic lipid content in hamsters fed high fat diets supplemented with white rice protein, brown rice protein, soy protein and their hydrolysates. J Agric Food Chem 2011, 59:10927-10933.

CHAPTER 4
PEA PROTEIN

INTRODUCTION

Pea protein hydrolysate is extracted from garden peas (Pisum sativum), which contain fleshy green/yellow seeds. Consumption of peas in their natural state does not necessarily result in the same health benefits as the protein hydrolysate because some potentially bioactive compounds or proteins are present in an inactive state in natural pea produce. Such active compounds are produced by the use of enzymatic digestion.

One principal and desirable effect of pea protein hydrolysate is the presence of compounds that act as ACE inhibitors. Inhibition may occur in the conversion of angiotensin I to the potent vasoconstrictor, angiotensin II, with resultant improvement of blood flow and lowering of blood pressure in humans.

PEA PROTEIN LOWERS BLOOD PRESSURE

Researchers at the University of Manitoba (Canada) have studied the effects of pea protein hydrolysate in hypertensive rats and humans and demonstrated blood pressure lowering effects (Li H, Prairie N, Udenigwe CC, et al, Journal of Agricultural and Food Chemistry, pre-published online, 2011 doi 10.1021/jf201911p). These investigators used rats that are genetically predisposed to hypertension (spontaneously hypertensive rats) and administered 100 and 200 mg per kg of body weight of pea protein. A maximum reduction of 19 mmHg in systolic blood pressure was noted four hours after consuming pea hydrolysate. In these experiments, pea protein in its natural state (non-hydrolyzed) had no significant effect on blood pressure.

In the experimental animals (Li et al, ibid, 2011), the administration of pea protein hydrolysate was associated with lower levels of angiotensin II and an approximate 50% reduction in renin, mRNA levels. In these studies, it was concluded that control of the output of renin by the kidneys, as a consequence of pea protein hydrolysate administration, resulted in lower levels of angiotensin II. This occurred as a direct consequence of alteration of the renin-angiotensin system.

Smaller reductions in blood pressure were noted in the human compared with the animal studies of pea protein isolate (Li, H., et al, ibid). In the human arm of the studies (Li H, et al, ibid, 2011), seven volunteers (age range 30-55 years, systolic blood pressure range 125-170 mmHg) had modest reductions in blood pressure as a consequence of the administration of 1.5 or 3.0g daily of pea protein hydrolysate over a three week period.

Pea protein has been found to have a potential role in reducing blood pressure and improving kidney function (Aluko R, 239th National Meeting of the American Chemical Society). In these studies, small doses of hydrolyzed pea protein administered to rats with polycystic kidney disease showed a 20% reduction in blood pressure. In addition, there were improvements in renal function, with a 30% increase in urine production. The mechanism of this beneficial action on renal function and blood pressure control may be related to the boosting of the production of cyclooxygenase-1 (COX-1), which may promote renal function.

OTHER PROPERTIES OF PEA PROTEIN

Studies in vitro (SIMPHYD) and in vivo show that pea protein is effective at inducing satiety with equivalence to whey protein (Ruijschop R, www.nizo.com/explore/cases, 2013, accessed Dec. 6, 2013). In vitro experiments reveal that pea protein agglomerates at its isoelectric point, but it does not engage in "network formation" like casein. The speed of digestion of pea protein is intermediate between casein (a slow protein) and whey (a fast protein). Measurement of patterns of gut hormone responses have shown only small differences following the administration of pea and whey protein meals. These findings imply that there are no major differences between pea and whey in terms of their propensity to cause alterations in satiety or weight gain by hormonal changes.

In general, dietary plant proteins exert influences on lipid metabolism in humans and animals. For example, soy protein has both hypocholesterolemic and hypotriglyceridemic effects that surpass the actions of casein (Spielman Gl et al, Journal of Animal Physiology and Animal Nutrition, 92, 683-93, 2008). Other plant proteins can reduce concentrations of cholesterol and triacylglycerols in rats, e.g. lupin derived protein (Sirtori et al, Journal of Nutrition, 134, 18-23, 2004).

Peas, soya and lupins have a relatively similar content of amino acids with a low content of methionine and a high concentration of arginine. Furthermore, the ratio of arginine to lysine is much higher in leguminous protein than found in casein. This ratio of arginine to lysine has been proposed as a significant factor in the hypocholesterolemic effect of both soy and lupin protein (Spielman Gl et al ibid, 2008).

Studies in pigs using whole peas in their natural state (P. sativum), show increased levels of very low density lipoproteins (VLDL) and low density lipoproteins. These findings were associated with an increased excretion of fecal steroids (Kingman et al, British Journal of Nutrition, 69, 409-21, 1993). In separate studies, whole raw peas fed to pigs who were on a high cholesterol diet caused lowering of blood cholesterol, LDL, and cholesterol levels in the liver. The complex composition of whole peas (starch, polysaccharides, and plant sterols) are also responsible for the individual effects of these different ingredients of whole peas on lipid metabolism.

Spielman Gl et al (ibid, 2008) have examined the effects of pure pea protein isolate in rats. Rats fed the purified pea protein diet had both a lower concentration of total cholesterol in the liver and VLDL than control animals fed a casein-rich diet. Further findings in this study included the ability of pea protein to stimulate the formation and excretion of bile acids in the liver, thereby reducing hepatic cholesterol concentration and reducing the secretion of cholesterol by actions on VLDL.

Studies of sterol regulating element-binding protein (SREBP)-2 and its target genes 3-hydroxy-3-methylglutary coenzyme A reductase (HMG-CoA) and LDL receptors in the liver reveal general increases in rats fed pea protein. These data suggest that gene expression of SREBP-2 and its target genes HMG-CoA and LDL receptors are involved in mechanisms whereby compensation occurs for an increased loss of cholesterol that is used for bile acid synthesis (Spielman et al, ibid, 2008).

Studies at the University of Toronto (Canada) have examined the effects of intact and hydrolyzed pea protein on food intake, glycemic response, and subjective appetite in healthy male volunteers (Luhovyy B, www.clinicaltrials.gov/show/NCT 01298154, accessed Dec. 6, 2013). In brief, it has been found that increasing pea protein leads to decreased blood glucose responses and reductions of food intake. Further research is recommended to define the effects of intact and hydrolyzed pea protein on glycemic responses and appetite in both pre and post-meal circumstances. The differences between intact and hydrolyzed pea protein requires detailed comparisons to be undertaken with other plant proteins, e.g. rice and soy, where outcomes have been better defined.

Recent studies in animals (rats) on a high cholesterol diet showed reductions of blood cholesterol after the administration combinations of pea protein with oat fiber or apple pectin (soluble fiber) (Parolini S, et al, British Journal of Nutrition, online print, doi 10.1017/50007114513000639). It is apparent that these rats showed better control of blood cholesterol with the combination of pea protein and oat fiber or apple pectin, compared with circumstances that result from the individual administration of pea protein or soluble fiber.

BENEFITS AND SAFETY OF PEA PROTEIN

It is clear that pea protein has major promise for the nutritional support of healthy blood pressure, lipid metabolism, and renal function. Pea protein hydrolysate is gluten free, hypoallergenic, and well tolerated (without gastrointestinal side effects). Elegant toxicological studies of pea protein isolate show that it is not genotoxic (Aouatif, C, et al, Hindawi Publishing Corporation, ISRN Toxicology, vol. 2013, Article ID 817353, DOI 10.115/2013/817353). Genotoxicity testing of pea protein in bacterial reverse mutation tests, chromosome alteration tests, and micronucleus testing were all negative (Aouatif, C, ibid, 2013).

Pea and other proteins have a propensity to cause a build-up of uric acid. Therefore, it has the potential to cause gout (a painful inflammatory condition in joints due to the build-up of uric acid). Individuals taking other protein supplements are potentially at risk of this disorder and it is very important to maintain adequate hydration to help avoid these side effects. With high dosages of plant proteins, calcium intake should be optimal to avoid calcium loss from bones, which may lead to osteoporosis.

CONCLUSION

Pea protein has found an increasing role in the addition to a variety of foods. It is beneficial by its positive effects on blood pressure regulation, renal function, satiety promotion and support of normal renal function.

PEA PROTEIN REFERENCES

Alonso, R.; Grant, G.; Marzo, F. 2001. Thermal treatment improves nutritional quality of pea seeds (*Pisum sativum* L.) without reducing their hypocholesterolemic properties. Nutrition Research, 21, 1067-1077.

Anderson, J.W.; Johnstone, B.M.; Cook-Newell, M.E. 1995. Meta-analysis of the effects of soybean protein intake on serum lipids. New England Journal of Medicine, 333, 276-282.

Aouatif, C.; Looten, Ph.; Parvathi, M.V.S.; et al. 2013. Genotoxicological Evaluation of NUTRALYS Pea Protein Isolate. Hindawi Publishing Corporation. http://dx.doi.org/10.1155/2013/817353.

Brown, M.S.; Kovanen, P.T.; Goldstein, J.L. 1981. Regulation of plasma cholesterol by lipoprotein receptors. Science, 212, 628-635.

Geraedts, M.C.P.; Troost, F.J.; Munsters, M.J.M.; Stegen, J.H.C.H.; de Ridder RJ; et al. 2011. Intraduodenal Administration of Intact Pea Protein Effectively Reduces Food Intake in Both Lean and Obese Male Subjects. PLoS ONE 6(9): e24878. Doi:10.1371/journal.pone.0024878.

Jacques, H.; Deshaies, Y.; Savoie, L. 1986. Relationship between dietary proteins, their *in vitro* digestion products, and serum cholesterol in rats. Atherosclerosis, 66, 89-98.

Kingman, S.M.; Walker, A.F.; Low, A.G.; Sambrook, I.E.; Owen, R.W.; Cole, T.J. 1993. Comparative effects of four legume species on plasma lipids and fecal steroid excretion in hypercholesterolemia pigs. The British Journal of Nutrition, 69, 409-421.

Kritchevsky, D.; Tepper, S.A.; Czarnecki, S.K.; Klurfeld, D.M. 1982. Atherogenicity of animal and vegetable protein. Influence of the lysine to arginine ratio. Atherosclerosis, 41, 429-431.

Martins, J.M.; Riottot, M.; de Abreu, M.C.; Lanca, M. J.; Viegas-Crespo, A.M.; Almeida, J.A.; Freire, J.B.; Bento, O.P. 2004. Dietary raw peas (*Pisum sativum* L.)

reduce plasma total and LDL cholesterol and hepatic esterified cholesterol in intact and ileorectal anastomosed pigs fed cholesterol-rich diets. Journal of Nutrition, 134, 3305-3312.

Matscheski, A.; Richter, D.U.; Hartmann, A.M.; Effmert, U.; Jeschke, U.; Kupka, M.S.; Abarzua, S.; Briese, V.; Ruth, W.; Kragl, U.; Piechulla, B. 2006. Effects of phytoestrogen extracts isolated from rye, green and yellow pea seeds on hormone production and proliferation of trophoblast tumor cells Jeg3. Hormone Research, 65, 276-288.

Morita, T.; Oh-Hashi, A.; Takei, K.; Ikai, M.; Ksaoka, S.; Kiriyama, S. 1996. Cholesterol-lowering effects of soybean, potato and rice proteins depend on their low methionine contents in rat fed a cholesterol-free purified diet. Journal of Nutrition, 127, 470-477.

Sirtori, C.R.; Galli, G.; Lovati, M.R.; Carrara, P.; Bosisio, E.; Kienle, M.G. 1984. Effects of dietary proteins on the regulation of liver lipoprotein receptors in rats. Journal of Nutrition, 114, 1493-1500.

Sirtori, C.R.; Lovati, M.R.; Manzoni, C.; Castiglioni, S.; Duranti, M.; Magni, C.; Morandi, S.; D'Agostina, A.; Arnoldi, A. 2004. Proteins of white lupin seed, a naturally isoflavone-poor legume, reduce cholesterolemia in rats and increase LDL receptor activity in HepG2 cells. Journal of Nutrition, 134, 18-23.

Spielmann, J., Stangl, G. I., Eder, K. 2008. Dietary pea protein stimulates bile acid excretion and lowers hepatic cholesterol concentration in rats. Institute of Agricultural and Nutritional Sciences, Martin-Luther-University of Halle-Wittenberg. DOI: 10.1111/j.1439-0396.2007.00766.x.

Sugano, M.; Ishiwaki, N.; Nakashima, K. 1984. Dietary protein-dependent modification of serum cholesterol level in rats. Significance of the arginine/lysine ratio. Annals of Nutrition and Metabolism, 28, 192-199.

Sugiyama, K.; Kanamori, H.; Akachi, T.; Yamakawa, A. 1996. Amino acid composition of dietary proteins affects plasma cholesterol concentration through alteration of hepatic phospholipid metabolism in rats fed a cholesterol-free diet. Journal of Nutritional Biochemistry, 7, 40-48.

Vlahcevic, Z.R.; Pandak, W.M.; Stravitz, R.T. 1999. Regulation of bile acid biosynthesis. Gastroenterology Clinics of North America, 28, 1-25.

CHAPTER 5
HEMP PROTEIN

HEMP: GENERAL INFORMATION

Hemp is derived most often from the Cannabis indica plant, (species of Cannabis indica). These plants grow as many variants (Holt S, The Cannabis Revolution, Author House, 2015). Hemp is a rich source of nutrients and it is gaining popularity as a source of functional foods and dietary supplements. Hemp protein applied for nutritional use is derived often from the seeds of Cannabis sativa or indica which are selected to not contain significant amounts of psychoactive substances (THC, the psychoactive cannabinoid). There are residual differences of opinion on how to classify different forms of the genus of Cannabis, but all forms contain variable amounts and types of cannabinoids with a predominant content of cannabidiol (CBD) in hemp versus marijuana. The most important classification systems involve the chemical characterization of the types and amounts of cannabinoid contents of the species of the plant. As described earlier, the whole family of plants are referred to as Cannabaceae, which includes the genus Cannabis and Humulus. There are considered to be three main species of Cannabis(C.), including C.-sativa, C. indica, and C. ruderalis.

As mentioned, cannabis contains two major cannabinoids; THC (delta-9 tetrahydrocannabinol) and CBD (cannabidiol). THC is the principal psychoactive component of mixed cannabinoids and CBD is known to modulate the central nervous system reactions to THC. However, CBD is highly versatile in several positive effects on body function. There has been an important recognition of two principal types of Cannabis, namely "drug (psychoactive) types" and preponderant "fiber types" (hemp). More detailed chemotypic (chemical content) classifications of Cannabis include 1) the more pure drug type (high in THC, often at a concentration of 2-6% or greater) and lacking in CBD, 2) an intermediate type (containing mainly THC with some CBD) and 3) a "fiber type" (with THC levels often less than 0.25% and variable CBD content). Some types of modern Cannabis sativa contain up to 20 percent concentration of THC (e.g. skunk, "Made In England").

Upon review, it is clear that industrial hemp is not considered to be marijuana. Marijuana is characteristically high in THC and low in CBD. Some uninformed individuals believe that permitting hemp to have legal status is tantamount to legalizing marijuana or facilitating its availability. This opinion is nonsense. In brief, using hemp-containing CBD that is low in THC has many health benefits and it will prevent the achievement of significant psychoactive reactions (the marijuana "high"). That said, the Food and Drug Administration have ruled that CBD (cannabidiol) cannot be sold as a dietary supplement (May 2015).

In 1970, the assent of the Comprehensive Drug Abuse and Prevention and Control Act superseded the earlier Marijuana Tax Act of 1937. The 1970 Tax Act made all Cannabis cultivation, including hemp, illegal in the U.S. Despite this ban in the U.S., there are at least 29 countries who permit the legal cultivation of hemp. The sale of hemp products is permitted in the U.S. for non-drug uses, e.g. in garments and as dietary protein sources, using appropriate types of hemp protein. On balance, I believe that a number of concerns expressed about certain foods of hemp origin are quite arbitrary and not supported by a review of scientific studies.

Hemp has been propagated by agricultural means to contain less than 0.3% THC, which is generally considered as the upper level of THC in hemp that is permissible, at law in the U.S.A. It is important to note that regulations on the sale of cannabis vary from country to country and now State to State in the U.S.A., but regulations concerning hemp use as a dietary or food supplement are quite confusing. Recent legislation in the U.S.A. is more permissive of hemp production which is governed currently at the State level (Farm Bill of 2014, revisions of 2013 Hemp Proposals).

HEMP AND NUTRITION: BRIEF OVERVIEW

Hemp seeds are a rich source of edible oils and high quality protein. The main constituents of hempseed are summarized in Table 17.

- Oils account for 45 percent by weight of hempseed.
- 80 percent of hempseed oils are in the form of essential fatty acids (EFA).

- EFA in hempseed oil are present as omega 3 and 6 fatty acids (linoleic, omega-6 and alpha linolenic, omega 3). Also present are gamma-linolenic acid and stearidonic acid.
- Proteins with high "edestin" components constitute about 30 percent by weight of hemp seed. The amino acid profile of hemp protein is considered arguably to be "complete" (all essential amino acids, with some present in limited amounts).

Table 17. Main constituents of hempseed oil. The omega 6 to omega 3 ratio of fatty acid content of the oil is approximately 3 to 1.

Thus, hemp seeds present a good source of high quality protein with a healthy content of EFA (essential fatty acids) in a desirable 3:1 omega fatty acid ratio (omega 6: omega 3).

CANNABIS IN THE FOOD CHAIN

Cannabis sativa and indica are important and ancient source of medicine, food, oil and fiber. Ripe seeds of hemp and meal (made from seeds) are well defined origins of dietary fiber and unsaturated fats (Callaway, J.C., Hempseed as a Nutritional Resource: An Overview, Euphytica, 140, 65-72, 2004). Table 18 shows a representative analysis of the nutritional content of hempseed.

	Whole Seed	Seed Meal
Oil (%)	35.5	11.1
Protein	24.8	33.5
Carbohydrates	27.6	42.6
Moisture	6.5	5.6
Ash	5.6	7.2
Energy (kJ/100g)	2,200	1,700
Total dietary fiber (%)	27.6	42.6

Digestible fiber	5.4	16.4
Non-digestible fiber	22.2	26.2

Table 18: Typical nutritional content (%) of hempseed[1] cv Finola. Reproduced from Callaway, 2004.

Hempseed is a valuable source of vitamins (E and B class) and minerals. Typical nutritional values for minerals and vitamins found in hempseed have been compiled from analysis of Finola (a Finnish variety of hemp) in studies that have been performed and reported by Callaway (ibid 2004). (Table 19)

Vitamin E	90.0
Thiamine (B1)	0.4
Riboflavin (B2)	0.1
Phosphorus (P)	1,160
Potassium (K)	859
Magnesium (Mg)	483
Calcium (Ca)	145
Iron (Fe)	14
Sodium (Na)	12
Manganese (Mn)	7
Zinc (Zn)	7
Copper (Cu)	2

TABLE 19: Typical nutritional values (mg/100g) for vitamins and minerals in hempseed[1] cv Finola. Reproduced from Callaway, 2004.

A striking property of hempseed is its high percentage of quality protein containing all essential amino acids. Callaway (ibid, 2004) has produced a very valuable study of the amino acid content of hemp and compared this with other food sources of protein. Table 20 shows this analysis combined with information taken from reliable studies (Callaway, ibid 2004, quotes work of Scherz et al Food Composition and Nutritional Tables 1986/1987, 3rd edition, Stuttgart).

Amino Acid	Potato (2%)	Wheat (14%)	Maize (11%)	Rice (9%)	Soy bean (32%)	Hempseed (25%)	Rapeseed (23%)	Egg white (13%)	Wh Pow (1?)
Alanine	0.09	0.50	0.72	0.56	1.39	1.28	1.05	0.83	0.
Arginine	0.10	0.61	0.40	0.62	2.14	3.10	1.49	0.68	0.
Aspartic Acid	0.34	0.69	0.60	0.86	3.62	2.78	1.82	1.23	1.
Cystine	0.02	0.28	0.15	0.10	0.54	0.41	0.39	0.29	0.
Glutamic Acid	0.37	4.00	1.80	1.68	5.89	4.57	4.41	1.67	2.
Glycine	0.10	0.71	0.35	0.47	1.29	1.14	1.28	0.50	0.
Histodine*	0.03	0.27	0.26	0.19	0.76	0.71	0.72	0.28	0.
Isoleucine*	0.08	0.53	0.35	0.35	1.62	0.98	1.00	0.74	0.
Leucine*	0.11	0.90	1.19	0.71	2.58	1.72	1.80	1.08	1.
Lysine*	0.10	0.37	0.33	0.31	1.73	1.03	1.49	0.74	1.
Methionine*	0.02	0.22	0.18	0.17	0.53	0.58	0.46	0.47	0.
Phenylalanine*	0.08	0.63	0.46	0.43	1.78	1.17	1.05	0.76	0.
Proline	0.09	1.53	0.85	0.40	1.65	1.15	1.59	0.50	0.
Serine	0.08	0.70	0.47	0.48	1.54	1.27	1.10	0.92	0.
Threonine*	0.07	0.42	0.34	0.34	1.35	0.88	1.13	0.58	1.
Tryptophan*	0.02	0.51	0.04	0.09	0.41	0.20	0.31	0.20	0.

Tyrosine	0.06	0.40	0.36	0.33	1.14	0.86	0.69	0.46	0.47
Valine*	0.10	0.61	0.46	0.51	1.60	1.28	1.26	0.98	0.91

TABLE 20: Typical protein content (%) of each food is given directly alongside the name. Individual amino acid values for each food is given in grams per 100 g. Essential amino acids are indicated by an asterisk (*). Reproduced from Callaway, 2004.

HEMP AND CANNABINOIDS

Hemp is a highly variable source of cannabidiol (CBD) in preponderant amounts (sometimes about 4 percent dry weight), but hempseed oil can contain negligible or smaller amounts of CBD. Hemp oil may contain traces of THC, usually less than 0.3 percent and it does not have any psychoactive properties. Less than a 0.3 percent concentration is the legal limit for hemp oil contents of THC. Many hybrids of Cannabis have been produced by special selection and growing techniques where CBD contents of hemp can be increased to about 14 percent CBD or more per dry weight of the hemp in question (e.g. Charlotte's web).

EFA AND PUFA IN HEMPSEED

Hempseed is a rich source of essential fatty acids. Approximately 56% of the fat in hempseed is LA (linoleic acid, omega 6) and 19% is LNA (linolenic acid, omega 3), which (provides LA (linoleic acid)/LNA (linolenic acid) in an optimal balance ratio of Omega 6 to Omega 3 fatty acids, in a 3:1 ratio. Thus, hempseed oil contains omega 3, 6, and 9 fatty acids (linoleic acid, LA, linolenic acid LNA and gamma linolenic acid GLA, respectively). Dietary inclusion of essential fatty acids (EFA) and polyunsaturated fatty acids (PUFA) are very important in the maintenance of human health. They control eicosanoid production and cause alterations in prostaglandin activity. These compounds play an important role in normal immune function with a special role in inflammatory and allergic disease. In addition, EFA and PUFA can exert a positive influence on reducing low density lipoproteins (LDL), thereby promoting cardiovascular health. Furthermore, there is some evidence that LA and LNA reduce the time required for muscle fatigue to recover following strenuous exercise.

HEMPSEED PROTEIN

Hempseed proteins are largely composed in two main types of protein, namely albumin and edestin which are globular and legumin type proteins, respectively. It is apparent that amino acid profiles of hempseed are comparable to other high quality proteins (e.g. egg whites and soy), (Table 20). Hemp protein is high in arginine, glutamic acid and sulfur-containing amino acids (cystine and methionine). Hemp is also comparatively high in tyrosine, alanine, and aspartic acid. While hemp has been portrayed as a complete protein, especially in advertising in sports nutrition, it has some potential limitations. Although hemp seeds and hemp oil from plants contain all essential amino acids, some are present in relatively small (limiting) amounts.

The limiting amino acid in hemp protein is lysine and to a lesser extent the amino acids leucine and L-tryptophan. That said, hemp protein has a good absorption profile and studies show that bioactive antioxidant peptides are produced from hemp protein (as studied in simulated digestive studies). In brief, hempseed meal has been reported to have a range of digestibility rating scores (from 50 to 86 percent approximately). Some studies have claimed a PDCAAS protein rating score of approximately 86-87% compared with 97% for casein, but hempseeds in different forms (oil extracted or dehulled seeds) may have lower PDCAAS scores. Some studies show protein in hempseed (whole seeds or meal) is only 50% digestible. This digestibility score rises to approximately 65% when the seed is dehulled.

HEALTH BENEFITS OF HEMPSEED

Studies in experimental animals (rodents) have shown that hempseed may have positive benefits on memory and learning, perhaps by activating calcineurin. In ovariectomised experimental rats, the use of 1-10% of hempseed in the diet has been shown to reduce experimental menopausal- related anxiety in a dose-dependent manner, probably as a result of its contents of specific phytonutrients.

Dietary additions of hempseed (up to 10% of a total meal) raises blood levels of omega 3 and 6 fatty acids with modest reductions in platelet aggregation. In other experiments in healthy individuals, 30ml of hempseed oil given with a "regular" diet for one month resulted in reductions in blood triglycerides without effects on LDL (or LDL-C). Other studies have shown similar outcomes, but not all studies have duplicated consistent effects on the lowering of blood triglycerides.

Oral intake of hempseed oil (30ml) over a period of eight weeks in patients with atopic dermatitis has resulted in a non-significant trend in reductions of trans-epidermal water loss, dryness, and itching. Furthermore, some studies suggest an effect of cannabidiol (CBD), within hemp oil, on selective cyclo-oxygenase type 2 inhibition, but these effects are small and unlikely to be of clinical significance. Other studies show that cannabidiol (and cannabidiolic acid) have anti-cancer properties in one type of invasive breast cancer; and these latter effects appear to be independent of any effects on COX-2 (cycto-oxygenase) enzymes.

Much of the alleged benefits of hemp protein focus on its potential role in the support of cardiovascular health, but detailed information on the actions of hemp protein to provide benefit in the prevention of myocardial infarction, hypertension, atherosclerosis, cardiac arrhythmias, and inflammatory states are required from future studies in both animals and humans. Promising data is emerging about the arginine content of hemp protein and its potential role as a nitric oxide precursor. The bioavailability and/or biological actions of key nutritional components of hemp protein (fatty acids, amino acids, and fiber) require considerable further exploration.

Whether or not hemp seed or hemp protein can be valuable in the prevention or management of other metabolic or cardiovascular co-morbidities (e.g. diabetes mellitus, metabolic syndrome, heart failure, etc.) remains underexplored (Rodriguez-Levva D. and Pirce, G.N., The cardiac and hemostatic effects of dietary hempseed, Nutr. Metab (London) 7, 32, DOI 101186/1743-7075-7-32, April 21, 2010). The most popular use of hemp protein in nutritional practice is found in sports nutrition.

THE CANNABIS PLANT GENOME

"The Genomic Research Initiative" is a research program at the University of Colorado that is working towards an analysis and genetic mapping of DNA in cannabis. These genomic initiatives involve a collection of DNA samples from cannabis grown in many geographic locations, on a worldwide basis. These DNA samples are being investigated to provide a blueprint that can pave the way to growing specific, high value plants. One principal research objective is to produce a greater source of cannabinoids and other cannabis components that may have special medicinal uses, but the genetic basis of the nutritional value of cannabis is also of interest.

The University of Colorado genomic research team is led by a brilliant researcher from Canada, Dr. Nolan Kane. Dr. Kane has stressed the need to identify genes chromosomes at an in-depth level. Earlier research (2011) has shown a sequence of the genome of Cannabis sativa in a somewhat preliminary and "unrefined manner". No doubt, one may expect genetic modification to involve itself in cannabis research at some stage, but the work at the University of Colorado is not part of any genetic engineering (GMO) project. In summary, the research is restricted to working only with existing genes in the plant.

HEMP: NUTRITIONAL SUMMARY

There are many nutritional advantages and characteristics of hemp food which are summarized in Table 21 below.

- More then 60 percent hemp contents are "essential" nutrients.
- Low allergenic potential.
- All essential amino acids (with limiting amino acids).
- Healthy essential fatty acid contents omega 3: omega 6 ratio balanced at 1 to 3.
- Stearidonic acid and gamma linolenic acid contents amplify benefits of other essential fatty acids.
- Hemp is a good source of cannabidiol (CBD) with versatile treatment effects.

- Hemp has valuable components e.g. magnesium, iron, potassium, dietary fiber, antioxidants (Vitamin E) and mixed phytonutrients.
- Useful addition to cooking with the ability to control blood cholesterol.
- A sustainable disease resistant crop.
- Eco-friendly requiring less water with non-depleting properties on soil.

Table 21. Some nutritional advantages of hemp containing foods.

EATING CANNABIS OR HEMP

Hemp foods are rapidly gaining popularity with a perception of their superior nutritional value (Table 22). The use of hemp in cooking has expanded in a significant manner and it has become particularly attractive in health conscious young people involved in aerobic fitness. Correspondents have referred to hemp as **"the new soy"** (Diane Walsh, cannabisdigest.ca/hemp-foods-every-diet/). Soy has many advantages as a healthy source of protein and other nutritional factors with valuable biological actions (Holt S, The Soy Revolution, Random House, 1998).

A preferred source of hemp in the diet is hemp seed which is now popular in many health food stores and progressive supermarkets. The heart of the hemp seed is called the "hemp nut" which is the healthful source of oils and protein. Hemp seeds are eaten often in a raw form as a cereal dish or in a sprouted form. However, many other hemp containing foods have emerged e.g. butters, hemp tofu, milk, tea, ground forms for baking, shakes, granola type bread, bagels, cookies and a variety of snack foods. Hemp seeds do not need fancy preparation, they can be eaten in a raw form and packaged in foil for convenience.

GROWING CANNABIS

In some locations in the U.S.A. hemp cultivation is allowed under the new "Farm Bill" (2013, 14). While these circumstances vary by State, they are more liberal in locations where recreational cannabis use is allowed (Colorado and Washington State). Differences in genetic make-up of different species of cannabis occur and selective cross-breeding is used to change plant characteristics with a focus on the manipulation of cannabinoid contents. This process is not the same as genetic engineering (GM) product production. It is not possible to cover agricultural methods of cannabis growing in this short book, but the world-wide web is loaded with this information. Would-be cultivators should look for reliable guidelines for safe growing practices.

A number of other factors are responsible for good cannabis growth. These factors include sophisticated nutrient and light applications during growth cycles. Propagation of cannabis plants is usually maintained in outdoor or indoor locations in well-selected soil. However, hydroponic and aeroponic nutrient and water delivery systems combined with advanced lighting technology are now commonly applied in cannabis growing operations.

As described earlier, the main species of Cannabis include three types, notably sativa, indica and ruderalis. The ruderalis type has the lowest concentrations of cannabinoids and indica is usually richer, at least in CBD content. Cannabis sativa is the plant with the highest levels of THC (the principal psychoactive component), but some forms of hemp belong to the genus and species, Cannabis sativa. That said, it is clear that cannabinoid contents of various species of plant vary by geographic location, growing conditions and many other factors. The results of their consumption on psychoactive effects can be "context specific" and depend on THC content, primarily.

Modern techniques of Cannabis propagation for recreational use often favor the use of sensimilla types of cannabis (in popular language). In this process of plant propagation, female plants are protected from pollination so that the development of seed pods can be avoided. This method of propagation results in greater yields of flowers and resin which are the principal origin of THC. The careful selection of different strains results in desired increases in THC or CBD levels, altered plant aroma, occurrence of shortened growth periods and different plant coloration. In brief, many selective breeding actions have produced a vast number of strains, with a vast number of meaningless names. Cannabis strains are sometimes sold with no description or an inaccurate description of their cannabinoid components, even by allegedly informed sales people in some cannabis dispensaries in Colorado and Washington State.

DRIVING THE QUEST FOR CANNABIS LEGALIZATION

Federal guidelines that support marijuana prohibition have been undermined. However, many physicians and the majority of the general public do not believe that cannabis is a drug mixture, without medical value and without a reasonable level of safety. As discussed earlier, favorable perceptions of cannabis safety and its medical benefits are driving its use. Recreational use of THC containing cannabis is increasing as more people become convinced about its social value and safety. It has been argued that public opinion has driven politicians to approve cannabis use without an optimal amount of research to confirm its safety and efficacy. However, there is still a cautious approach to marijuana use, especially in the presence of data which indicate that its use in youngsters may result in a generation of adults with variable degrees of social or other disabilities. Most people are starting to view hemp as legal for growing and consuming in the U.S.A., but weakening arguments question the legality of hemp use.

CONCLUSION

Hemp has formed the basis of dietary supplements and food additives in many new brands and formats. This circumstance remains challenged somewhat by Federal regulators. Hemp is nutritious and has medicinal qualities as a useful functional food. The CBD (cannabidiol) content of hemp oil could present some problems because of the U.S Food and Drug Administration's statements that CBD is not a dietary supplement.

HEMP PROTEIN REFERENCES

Al-Khalifa A, Maddaford TG, Chahine MN, Austria JA, Edel AL, Richard MN, Ander BP, Gavel N, Kopilas M, Ganguly R, Ganguly PK, Pierce GN. Effect of dietary hempseed intake on cardiac ischemia-reperfusion injury. Am J Physiol Regul Integr Comp Physiol. 2007;292:R1198–203.

Callaway J, Schwab U, Harvima I, Halonen P, Mykkänen O, Hyvönen P, Järvinen T. Efficacy of dietary hempseed oil in patients with atopic dermatitis. J Dermatolog Treat. 2005;16:87–94. doi: 10.1080/09546630510035832.

Callaway, J.C., 2002. Hemp as food at high latitudes. J Ind Hemp 7(1): 105-117.

Callaway JC. Hempseed as a nutritional resource: An overview. Euphytica. 2004;140:65–72. doi: 10.1007/s10681-004-4811-6.

Callaway, J.C., T. Tennila & D.W. Pate, 1997a. Occurrence of *"omega*-3" stearidonic acid (*cis*-6,9,12,15-octadecatetraenoic acid) in hemp (*Cannabis sativa* L.) seed. J Int Hemp Assoc 3:61-63.

Callaway, J.C., & T.T. Laakkonen, 1996. Cultivation of *Cannabis* oil seed varieties in Finland. J Int Hemp Assoc 3(1): 32-34.

Darshan, S.K., & I.L. Rudolph, 2000. Effects of fatty acids of w-6 and w-3 type on human immune status and role of eicosanoids. Nutrition 16: 143-145.

Deferne, J.L. & D.W. Pate, 1996. Hemp seed oil: A source of valuable essential fatty acids. J Int Hemp Assoc 3(1): 1-7.

Dupasquier CMC, Weber AM, Ander BP, Rampersad PP, Steigerwald S, Wigle JT, Mitchell RW, Kroeger EA, Gilchrist JSC, Moghadasian MM, Lukas A, Pierce GN. The effects of dietary flaxseed on vascular contractile function and atherosclerosis in rabbits during prolonged hypercholesterolemia. Am J Physiol. 2006;291:H2987–H2996.

Goyens PL, Spilker ME, Zock PL, Katan MB, Mensink RP. Conversion of alpha-linolenic acid in humans is influenced by the absolute amounts of alpha-linolenic acid and linoleic acid in the diet and not by their ratio. Am J Clin Nutr. 2006;84:44–53.

Grigoriev, O.V., 2002. Application of hempseed (*Cannabis sativa* L.) oil in the treatment of the ear, nose and throat (ENT) disorders. J Ind Hemp 7(2): 5-15.

Hampson, A.J., M. Grimaldi, M. Lolic, D. Wink, R. Rosenthal, J. Axelrod, 2000. Neuroprotective antioxidants from marijuana. ANN N Y Acad Sci 899: 274-282.

Holler JM, Bosy TZ, Dunkley CS, Levine B, Past MR, Jacobs A. Delta9-tetrahydrocannabinol content of commercially available hemp products. J AnalToxicol. 2008;32:428–32.

Horia E, Watkins BA. Comparison of stearidonic acid and alpha-linolenic acid on PGE2 production and COX-2 protein levels in MDA-MB-231 breast cancer cell cultures. J Nutr Biochem. 2005;16:184–92. doi: 10.1016/j.jnutbio.2004.11.001.

Horrobin, D.F., 2000. Essential fatty acid metabolism and its modification in atopic eczema. Am J Clin Nutr 71(1): 367-72S.

Kaul N, Kreml R, Austria JA, Richard MN, Edel AL, Dibrov E, Hirono S, Zettler ME, Pierce GN. A comparison of fish oil, flaxseed oil and hempseed oil supplementation on selected parameters of cardiovascular health in healthy volunteers. J Am Coll Nutr. 2008;27:51–8.

Kinosian B, Glick H, Preiss L, Puder KL. Cholesterol and coronary heart disease: predicting risks in men by changes in levels and ratios. J Investig Med. 1995;43:443–450.

Kriese, U., E. Schumann, W.E. Weber, M. Beyer, L. Bruhl & B. Matthaus, 2004. Oil content, tocopherol composition and fatty acid patterns of the seeds of 51 *Cannabis sativa* L. genotypes. Euphytica 137: 339-351.

Laakkonen, T.T. & J.C. Callaway, 1998. Update on FIN-314. J Int Hemp Assoc 5(1): 34-35.

Leson, G., P. Pless & J.W. Roulac (Eds.), 1999. Hemp Foods & Oils for Health, 2nd edn. Hemptech, Ltd, Sebastopol.

Leson, G., P. Pless, F. Grotenhermen, H. Kalant & M.A. ElSohly, 2001. Evaluating the impact of hemp food consumption on workplace drug tests. J Anal Toxicol 25(8): 691-698.

McPartland, M.J. & G. Geoffrey, 2004. Random queries concerning the evolution of *Cannabis* and coevolution with the cannabinoid receptor. In: G. Guy, R. Robson, K. Strong & B. Whittle (Eds.), The Medicinal Use of Cannabis, pp. 71-102. Royal Society of Pharmacists, London.

Mechoulam, R., 1986. Cannabinoids as therapeutic agents, pp. 1-20. CRC Press, Boca Raton.

Mechoulam, R., D. Panikashvili & E. Shohami, 2002. Cannabinoids and brain injury: Therapeutic implications. Trends Mol Med 8(2): 58-61.

Mensink RP, Zock PL, Kester AD, Katan MB. Effects of dietary fatty acids and carbohydrates on the ratio of serum total to HDL cholesterol and on serum lipids and apolipoproteins: a meta-analysis of 60 controlled trials. Am J Clin Nutr. 2003;77:1146–55.

Mustafa, A.F., J.J. McKinnon & D.A. Christensen, 1999. The nutritive value of hemp meal for ruminants. Can J Anim Sci 79(1): 91-95.

Odani, S. & S. Odani, 1998. Isolation and primary structure of a methionine and cystine-rich seed protein of Cannabis sativa L. Biosci Biotechnol Biochem, 62: 650-654.

Prociuk M, Edel A, Gavel N, Deniset J, Ganguly R, Austria J, Ander B, Lukas A, Pierce G. The effects of dietary hempseed on cardiac ischemia/reperfusion injury in hypercholesterolemic rabbits. Exp Clin Cardiol. 2006;11:198–205.

Prociuk MA, Edel AL, Richard MN, Gavel NT, Ander BP, Dupasquier CM, Pierce GN. Cholesterol-induced stimulation of platelet aggregation is prevented by a hempseed-enriched diet.Can J Physiol Pharmacol. 2008;86:153–9. doi: 10.1139/Y08-011.

Richard MN, Ganguly R, Steigerwald SN, Al-Khalifa A, Pierce GN. Dietary hempseed reduces platelet aggregation. J Thromb Haemost. 2007;5:424–5. doi: 10.1111/j.1538-7836.2007.02327.x.

Ross SA, Mehmedic Z, Murphy TP, Elsohly MA. GC-MS analysis of the total 9-THC content of both drug-and fiber-type cannabis seeds. J Anal Toxicol. 2000;24:715–717.

Salonen JT, Salonen R, Ihanainen M, Parviainen M, Seppänen R, Kantola M, Seppänen K, Rauramaa R. Blood pressure, dietary fats, and antioxidants. Am J Clin Nutr. 1988;48:1226–1232.

Schwab US, Callaway JC, Erkkilä AT, Gynther J, Uusitupa MI, Järvinen T. Effects of hempseed and flaxseed oils on the profile of serum lipids, serum total and lipoprotein lipid concentrations and haemostatic factors. Eur J Nutr. 2006;45:470–7. doi: 10.1007/s00394-006-0621-z.

Simopoulos, A.P., 1999. Essential fatty acids in health and chronic disease. Am J Clin Nutr 70: 560-569.

Small, E. & D. Marcus, 2003. Tetrahydrocannabinol levels in hemp (*Cannabis sativa*) germplasm resources. Econ Bot 57(4): 545-558.

West DP. Hemp and Marijuana: Myths & Realities. North American Industrial Hemp Council, INC; 1998. http://www.votehemp.com/PDF/myths_facts.pdf April 8,2009.

Xiaozhai, L. & R.C. Clarke, 1995. The cultivation and use of hemp (*Cannabis sativa* L.) in ancient China. J Int Hemp Assoc 2(1): 26-33.

Zias, J., H. Stark, J. Sellgman, R. Levy, E. Werker, A. Breuer & R. Mechoulam, 1993. Early medicinal use of cannabis. Nature 363(6426): 215.

CHAPTER 6
SOY PROTEIN

INTRODUCTION

In brief, we have noted that surveys in the USA show that adult females in the U.S. have an average approximate protein intake of 55-62 grams per day, whereas males consume an average of approximately 70-100 grams of protein per day. In developed nations, up to 70% of the total human dietary intake of protein is derived from animal sources, which include meat, poultry, and fish. However, in the past 30 years there has been an increase in the use of soyfoods and other plant proteins in human diets ("The Soy Revolution," Holt, S. Dell Publishing, 1999).

In review, preferences for an increased dietary intake of vegetable or cereal proteins has emerged with the recognition that high protein intakes of animal origin have been definitively associated with an increase in the prevalence of certain chronic diseases. Factors that contribute to the development of chronic disease with animal protein diets include: the high intake of saturated fat, cooking techniques that generate heterocyclic amines (carcinogens) and the complete absence of dietary fiber in meat protein. Some studies have implied that after controlling for certain types of fat intake, protein per se does not increase the risk of heart disease. However, there is a clear link between cancer occurrence and total meat intake in the diet.

As mentioned earlier, beneficial health implications are at the basis of strong recommendations to obtain more protein in the diet from plants ("the Plant Protein Revolution"). Soy protein has paved the way for increased plant protein intake in general and it is now a ubiquitous ingredient in a variety of foods including: hot dogs, burgers, tofu, tempeh, miso, soy nuts, soy butter and soy milk. General health benefits are obvious and readily demonstrable (e.g. lowering of blood cholesterol) with soy inclusion in the diet at a level of 25 grams of soy protein per day (and also conditionally at 6.25 grams per day).

SOY PROTEIN: BRIEF OVERVIEW

Soy (soya) protein can be readily extracted from soybeans. Protein is stored in soybeans in particles (protein bodies) which contain up to three quarters of the total protein content of a soybean. Soy protein is a complete protein with its content of all essential amino acids. In common with several other plant proteins, the soybean has been modified by genetic engineering to improve growth characteristics, resistance to herbicides and boost certain nutritional components.

Soy protein has been used for about 60 years to improve the physico-chemical properties of food. Such improvements include favorable alterations in food texture and emulsifying properties. The health properties of soy protein and soyfoods are legion. It has been used in the management of a variety of disorders, notably: high blood cholesterol and or blood pressure; prevention of heart and blood vessel disease (atherosclerosis); type 2 diabetes mellitus; asthmatic disorders, and cancer of the lung, uterus, prostate and thyroid. Other general benefits of soyfoods include: osteoporosis prevention, improvements in certain causes of diminished renal function, e.g. to cause diminishing proteinuria. Soy protein has been used extensively in sports nutrition with reports of its ability to improve lean muscle mass and assist in relieving muscle soreness following exercises.

Phytoestrogens (isoflavones, daidzein, genistein and glycetein) in soy have perceived benefits and disadvantages. Soy has found specific applications in women's health for managing mastalgia (breast pain and tenderness) and it may play an important role in breast cancer prevention. Soy supplements and food containing isoflavones has been used to variably control symptoms of menopause, e.g. hot flashes and it may be valuable in the symptomatic management of premenstrual syndrome (PMS). Soy has played a special role as an alternative to dairy milk supplements in infant formulae and soymilk has gained increasing popularity in all age groups.

It should be recognized that conflicting data exist in research studies with soy in certain circumstances of health promotion. There has been much debate about the safety of isoflavones that are contained within soy. These bioactive components of soy are often estrogenic in their actions in humans (phytoestrogens). Moreover, there is much difference of opinion in their ability to induce favorable effects in certain conditions, such as control of menopausal symptoms and cancer prevention.

SOY PROTEIN: TYPES AND HEALTH CLAIMS

Soy protein is manufactured from soybeans in different ways, resulting in essentially three types of "processed soy," namely: 1) Soy protein isolate (SPI), 2) Soy protein concentrate (SPC), and 3) Textured soy protein (TSP). In brief, TSP is made from SPC by producing chips, dry flakes or chunks and in common with SPC it contains about 70-80% total protein. Soy protein concentrate (SPC) is crude soy protein from which water soluble carbohydrates and other soluble compounds have been removed. Moreover, SPI is the highest concentration of refined (highly processed) soy protein, with a protein concentration of about 90%. In recent years, there has been a dramatic increase in the use of soy protein isolates as food additives. This trend has been criticized by some scientists who point out the loss of many health-giving nutrients as a consequence of the extensive processing of SPI. With some types of undesirable soyfood manufacturing techniques, there is an uncommon possibility of residual contents of potentially toxic agents in SPI such as aluminum and hexane or the residual presence of anti-nutrients.

There has been a significant amount of confusion about health claims for soy. Soy protein health claims are allowable under the following circumstances: 1) A serving of the product in question may contain only a maximum of 3 grams of fat, unless the product is derived from whole soy and there has been no added fat, 2) The product must be low in sodium (< 480 mg of sodium in individual foods, < 720 mg of sodium in a main dish, < 960 mg of sodium in a total meal product) and low in cholesterol (< 20 mg cholesterol), and 3) One serving of the product in question must contain at least 6.25 grams of soy protein. This information constitutes the "conditional" soy for health claim.

ISOFLAVONES: GENERAL CONCEPTS

The principal soy isoflavones are genstein, daidzein, and glycetein (genistin, daidzin, and glycetin). The consequences or benefits of isoflavones are dependent on continuous intake of soy foods in the diet. However, there is *inconsistent* consumption of soy foods among Westerners and there is great variability in the isoflavone content of soy foods.

Food processing techniques that use solvents (e.g., aqueous alcoholic solutions or hexane) may remove isoflavones from soy foods, thereby making the total isoflavone content unpredictable. Thus, it is difficult to give dietary advice to permit an individual to ingest the optimal amount of isoflavones. For the most part, most Westerners find it unacceptable to eat eight to ten ounces (more than one half pound) of tofu per day. This is the amount of "average" tofu that has to be eaten in one day in order to ingest 50 to 80 mg of isoflavones per day (a range of dosage of isoflavones with significant bioactivity).

Post-marketing surveillance studies have shown that it is common to find mislabeled amounts of isoflavones in soy foods. Not all tofu is created equal, and nutritionists or other health care givers and consumers have sought ways to obtain predictable amounts of isoflavones that will produce the optimal health outcome. This reasoning has supported the use of isoflavone containing dietary supplements that are made from fractions of soy.

Soy milk represents a practical alternative to dairy milk and is relatively easy to add to the diet. Quality milk products contain about 12 mg of total isoflavones per 100 ml, and 400 ml of soy milk per day is a very good health drink for mature men and women. However, some forms of soy milk contain only small amounts of isoflavones. Other convenient soy isoflavone supplements come in the form of soy protein isolate powders. Powdered, miscible beverages based on soy protein and isoflavone concentrates that can be combined with water or milk are also available.

THE VERSATILE ISOFLAVONES

Soy isoflavones have versatile biological effects, and their actions in the body are well-defined. Isoflavones can exert estrogenic (phytoestrogens) and antioxidant effects. The isoflavone genistein has antiangiogenic activity (interference with blood vessel growth). Antiangiogenesis is an important, potential cancer-fighting property. Isoflavones are known to inhibit enzymes that promote the growth of several types of cancer. In laboratory experiments, isoflavones have been shown to suppress variably the growth of many types of cancers of human and animal origin. The estrogen-modulating effects of soy isoflavones account for their potential, but arguable, benefit in managing symptoms of menopause, premenstrual syndrome, prostate disease, and estrogen-modulated cancers.

There are several hypothesized modes of action of isoflavones. Estrogenic hormones react with estrogen receptors in cells. Soy isoflavones are capable of binding with these receptors producing different degrees of estrogenic effects; and they provide generally a weaker estrogenic drive than the body's own estrogens. When isoflavones attach to the receptors, they can stimulate estrogenic actions or minimize, or weaken, the effects of the body's estrogen (when estrogen levels are high). In other words, in states of estrogen excess, isoflavones exert an antiestrogenic effect by reducing the access of the body's powerful estrogenic hormones to the receptor sites. In contrast, when estrogen is lacking, soy isoflavones are proestrogenic in their action. Thus, isoflavones *modulate* the action of estrogen, and they can be proestrogenic or antiestrogenic, depending on the circumstances of prevailing estrogen dominance, or lack thereof.

The "soy protein hypothesis" that relates to effects of increased dietary intake of soy protein and reductions of LDL was tested extensively in the 1970s and 80s. It had been proposed earlier by several researchers that soy had a direct cholesterol-lowering effect in humans. This effect was opposite to the rises in blood cholesterol that are variably encountered with animal protein intake in both animals and humans. That said, the ability of soy food to lower cholesterol in a significant manner remains challenged by recent research reviewed later in this chapter of the book.

CANCER PREVENTION

There are several well-designed population studies that demonstrate the role of soy isoflavones in cancer prevention. Many scientific studies show that vegetarians and Asians, who have a low incidence of breast and prostate cancer, are known to excrete high concentrations of phytoestrogens, notably isoflavones. The lower incidence of breast cancer in Singapore and Hong Kong has been directly linked to dietary intake of soy, with isoflavones identified as being the principal agents responsible for the reduced risk. Many other studies of Asian populations also link a lower risk for other types of cancer to their consumption of soy foods.

In several studies, a reduced risk of prostate cancer among Asian populations has been linked to soy isoflavone intake. Separate studies imply the same benefit of isoflavones in lung cancer and cancers affecting the gastrointestinal tract. However, some scientists are not convinced about cancer preventative effects of isoflavones and continue to argue that population studies are based on observation and do not provide "cast-iron" evidence of a cause-and-effect relationship between dietary soy intake and cancer prevention.

FOCUS ON GENISTEIN

The phenolic group of genistein permits it to act as an estrogen, but the double bond of the molecule (hydroxyl group 5, hydroxy-keto constituents) on the A and C ring of genistein permits it to act as an antiproliferative agent (meaning that it stops cell division and inhibits cancer growth). Some of the effects of soy isoflavones as anticancer agents seem to be related to nonestrogen-receptor mediated activity. Soy isoflavones interfere with molecules that promote cancer growth, inhibiting the effects of enzymes (protein tyrosine kinase inhibition) and growth factors (epidermal growth factor). They also act as an inhibitor of the growth-regulating enzymes (*e.g.*, DNA topoisamerase), which are responsible for apoptosis. These effects occur at one micromolar to ten micromolar concentrations of genistein. These are concentrations that are achievable with substantial soy intake or dietary supplementation of soy isoflavones.

Genistein is a specific inhibitor of aromatase enzymes and 17 beta hydroxyl steroid hydrogenase, which are enzymes that promote the production of estrogens from precursors in the body. It is recognized that Asian women living on soy-based diets often have about half the circulating concentrations of estradiol and estrone than Western women not on soy diets. In summary, genistein and perhaps daidzein may act as estrogen agonists, and their anticancer effects (antiproliferative effects) are due, in part, to their actions other than their estrogenic effects.

SOY AND HEALTHY BONES

Osteoporosis is a common disease among the elderly in Western industrialized countries. Unfortunately, to date there is no safe and completely effective treatment for this disease once it is well established. The most common type of osteoporosis is associated with bone loss in post-menopausal women. The estrogenic properties of soy isoflavones and some other plant products, such as lignins, have been investigated for their potential to treat and prevent osteoporosis. Based on evidence to date, using isoflavones for this purpose may be variably effective.

Several double-blind placebo-controlled clinical trials have shown that semisynthetic isoflavones, notably ipriflavone, are capable of increasing bone density in post-menopausal women. Ipriflavone is approved for prescription use in the treatment of osteoporosis in Europe, but not in the United States. When ipriflavone is administered to humans it is converted in part to daidzein, which is a key isoflavone. Several studies show that the addition of soy protein containing isoflavones can assist in the treatment of osteoporosis by increasing bone density in women with post-menopausal bone loss.

Several landmark studies have been performed on the relationship between animal protein-rich diets and calcium metabolism, especially in relationship to the formation of kidney stones. In these studies, individuals consumed diets containing varying amounts of calcium and protein of either plant or animal origin. Experimental subjects who consume animal protein may lose about 50 percent more calcium in their urine than those subjects who ate soy protein alone. The reason that soy protein isolates may protect against calcium loss from the body and renal stones are not entirely clear, but are probably related to their amino acid content.

ISOFLAVONES AND CARDIOVASCULAR HEALTH

Evidence exists that soy isoflavones can contribute to lowering blood cholesterol levels and inhibit the development of hardening of the arteries (atherosclerosis). The soy isoflavone, genistein, has been shown to directly inhibit several metabolic events that are involved in the cause of atherosclerosis. As for the ability of soy foods to lower cholesterol, dozens of studies performed over a period of seventy years form a body of convincing evidence that soy protein, containing isoflavones, lowers blood cholesterol efficiently. James Anderson, M.D., and his colleagues published their important work on the cholesterol-lowering effects of soy in the *New England Journal of Medicine* in 1995, but many physicians have been slow to incorporate these findings into their medical practices. More recent studies, however, have questioned the efficiency of soy protein for lowering blood lipids.

ANTIOXIDANTS AND ISOFLAVONES

Isoflavones mop up free radicals and act as antioxidants. A free radical is a molecule that is missing an electron, making it highly reactive. The molecule's unpaired electron seeks another electron, and the process starts again. Eventually, the continuous creation of free radicals damages genetic material or membranes in the cells of the body. Free radicals are a by-product of oxidation and are implicated in the cause of many diseases, including cancer and cardiovascular diseases. Free radicals are also implicated in other conditions associated with aging, such as skin wrinkling, cataracts and macular degeneration, etc. The delivery of plant protein with associated antioxidant contents is an obvious and positive health intervention with wide reaching potential.

SOY PROTEIN AND KIDNEY FUNCTION

Evidence has accumulated showing that vegetable-based protein, particularly soy protein, is much more efficiently handled by the kidneys than animal protein. Beneficial effects of soy diets on high blood cholesterol in patients with kidney impairment due to nephrotic syndrome have been reported. Nephrotic syndrome is a kidney disease that results in protein loss in the urine with variable degrees of water retention (edema), high blood pressure (hypertension), and high levels of fats in the blood (blood lipids). It has been found that switching from a predominately animal protein source to a vegetarian (soy) source of protein results in a substantial decrease in both blood cholesterol and protein loss from the kidneys in individuals with this and other types of kidney failure.

Studies of kidney, metabolic, and hormonal responses to animal and vegetable protein diets show that considerable benefits may result from vegetable protein-based diets. It has been found that animal protein causes an increase in glomerular filtration rate (the filtering mechanism of the kidneys) that is about one-fifth higher than that caused by soy protein. These studies imply that instead of making drastic reductions in protein intake in patients with kidney failure, it may be possible to switch the protein sources in the diet from animal to soy-based protein. Since kidney function decreases with age, soy protein is an attractive option as a source of protein for the diets of the elderly.

PROSTATIC DISEASE AND SOY

Several studies have drawn attention to the lower incidence of prostatic disease in Japanese men compared with Western men. The difference is particularly clear in older men. The difference in prevalence of prostatic disease has been ascribed in part to the high intake of soy foods in the Japanese diet. The isoflavone content of soy (genistein and daidzein) has been shown to directly affect testosterone metabolism and to help reduce the formation of toxic types of testosterone. The benefits of soy-based diets in the promotion of prostatic health have led to the recommendation that men at risk of prostate problems take soy daily in their diet.

SOY AND HYPERTENSION

Japanese investigators have shed some light on the antihypertensive effects of soybean diets. Studies have shown that fermented soy foods, such as natto and miso, may contain antihypertensive peptides that may interfere with blood pressure regulation. It appears that these peptides may interfere with angiotensin-converting enzyme, an enzyme that promotes the production of angiotensin, which, in turn, causes elevated blood pressure.

UNDESIRABLE CONTENTS OF SOY PROTEIN

It has been stated repeatedly that fermented soy products (tempeh, natto, miso, and soy condiments) are healthier than regular soy products, by virtue of a lower content of naturally occurring "toxins" or anti-nutritive compounds. The most significant "potentially toxic" compounds in soy include: phytic acid, trypsin inhibitors and sometimes aluminum and lysinoalanine.

Phytic acid is an example of an anti-nutrient in soy that can block the absorption of certain minerals such as calcium, magnesium, copper, iron, and zinc (Stipanuk, M., Biological, Physiological and Molecular Aspects of Nutrition, 2006). This has led to some claims that soy induced mineral deficiencies may cause health problems, e.g. zinc deficiency, reduced immune function, and potential for growth problems in children and pregnancy.

Important anti-nutrient components of soybeans and soy protein include trypsin inhibitors that have been associated with gastric distress and varying degrees of amino acids malabsorption. While trypsin inhibitors can be removed to a significant degree by high temperature processing, this practice may contribute to soy protein denaturation.

Heavy metal contamination is uncommon in soy food, but the use of aluminum tanks during some past manufacturing has been associated with contamination. Aluminum has neurotoxic properties and its presence has been associated with the development of pre-senile dementia (cf, Alzheimer's disease).

EDAMAME

Edamame consists of young soybeans that have been harvested before hardening of the beans. This highly nutritive food is a complete source of protein and it contains valuable amounts of iron and calcium in the absence of any cholesterol. The beans are high in omega 3 fatty acids (alphalinolenic acid) and one cup (155 grams) contains 189 calories consisting of 8 grams of fat, 16 grams of carbohydrate and 17 grams of protein.

In common with many other types of bean protein foods, edamame can reduce risks of cardiovascular disease. Moreover edamame may exert favorable effects on age related brain disease, cancer of the breast and colon, depression, diabetes mellitus, fertility, energy levels, inflammation and osteoporosis (adapted from www.medicalnewstoday.com/articles/280285.php, accessed May 2, 2015.

QUESTIONING HEALTH BENEFITS OF SOY

Early statements that soy can prevent cardiovascular disease (Code of Federal Regulations 21CFR 101.82,2001) have been questioned by contemporary studies (Saks FM et al American Heart Association scientific advisory for professionals from the nutrition committee, Circulation, 2006). Anderson JW et al (N.Engl. T. Med, 333, 276-82, 1995) undertook a metanalysis study which showed that eating about 50 grams of soy protein as a substitute for animal protein reduced total blood cholesterol by 9.3 percent, LDL cholesterol by 12.9 percent and triglycerides by 10.5 percent. More recent research by the American Heart Association's nutrition committee showed only a 3 percent reduction of LDL as a consequence of eating 50 grams of soy protein per day. That said, soy protein is still considered better for the promotion of cardiovascular health than meat protein.

While several studies have shown that soy isoflavones may be valuable in post menopausal hot flashes and other problems, the AHA committee has concluded that soy is not valuable in treating hot flashes or other negative symptoms of menopause (www.hsph.harvard.edu/nutrition source). One of the problems in some of these studies is compliance with the large amounts of soyfood that may be required to quell hot flashes and insufficient amounts of soy isoflavones given in dietary supplements to induce a phyto-estrogenic effect.

On the one hand some studies have shown a protective effect of soy on breast cancer, but on the other, no such effect can be demonstrated. While soy isoflavones may be expected to stimulate breast tissue in growth cycles, the weak estrogenic actions of soy may serve to block high endogenous estrogenic drive. As stated earlier, soy may sometimes exert an anti-estrogenic effect.

Moreover, the timing of soy ingestion may play a special role in the effects of isoflavones on breast health. For example, the Shanghai Women's Health Study reported that women with the highest soy protein intakes during adolescence and early adult life had almost a 60 percent lower risk of premenopausal breast cancer compared with women with the lowest intake of soy (Lee S A et al Am J. Clin Nutr, 89, 1920-1, 2009). Some authorities and researchers claim that soy has no preventive benefits for cancer of the prostate, colo-rectum, ovary and endometrium, but opinions differ.

Some studies have reported that soy consumption may assist in the prevention of age related memory loss or decline in cognitive function. Again there are studies with conflicting results in these areas of brain function. Furthermore, some studies imply that soy intake may lead to memory disorders. In one study, older females of Japanese descent who were domiciled in Hawaii appeared more likely to have cognitive problems than women who had switched to a Western diet (White L R et al J. Am. Coll. Nutr. 19, 242-55, 2000). The reasons for the conflicting data in these studies is not clear and further longitudinal research studies are required.

A REVIEW OF PROBLEMS WITH SOY PROTEIN SUPPLEMENTATION

The most significant problem with soy protein is the occurrence of allergy which can take a form ranging from simple digestive upset to severe allergic responses. Some components of soy e.g. lectins have been implicated in the cause of indigestion which is the commonest form of digestive upset reported in soy food consumers. In general, fermented soy foods are better tolerated than unfermented versions of this food. Unfortunately soy supplement powders are not often available in fermented forms.

The presence of isoflavones in soy, namely genistein, daidzein and glycetein often causes debate about the safety of soy. Isoflavones are weak estrogens that have an overall effect on estrogen dominance in the body. The estrogenic drive provided by isoflavones has been perhaps overemphasized because the isoflavones are estrogen modulators not just simple estrogens. This makes isoflavones somewhat desirable for females.

As noted earlier, an isoflavone can occupy and estrogen receptor and the presence of excessive estrogen it has a down regulating effect on estrogenic status. In contrast, when estrogen is lacking the isoflavone cuts as an estrogen agonist, even though the estrogenic potency of isoflavones are less than naturally occurring estrogen.

Soy intake has been associated with the development of thyroid disorders by virtue of its content of a goitrogen that can suppress thyroid function. However, the occurrence of thyroid disease and goiter (enlargement of the gland) are disputed by some. Much controversy has emerged about the role, if any, of soy isoflavones in the cause of breast cancer. However, many studies imply that soy food does not give rise to breast cancer. Soy protein can improve muscle mass as a protein supplement and it acts to variably lower blood cholesterol (LDL) and variably provide symptomatic relief for women experiencing the transition of menopause.

CONCLUSION

Soy protein has clear health benefits, some of which are questioned by contemporary research.

REFERENCES

Ahsan N, Komatsu S. Comparative analyses of the proteomes of leaves and flowers at various stages of development reveal organ specific functional differentiation of proteins in soybean. Proteomics. 2009;9(21):4889–4907. doi: 10.1002/pmic.200900308.

American Dietetic Association and Dieticians of Canada (ADA) 2000. Manual of clinical dietetics (6th ed.) Chicago: ADA and Dieticians of Canada.

Anderson J. J, Chen X, Boass A, Symons M, Kohlmeier M, Renner J. B, Garner S. C. Soy isoflavones: No effects on bone mineral content and bone mineral density in healthy, menstruating young adult women after one year. Journal of the American College of Nutrition. 2002;388-393. (PubMed).

Anderson J. W, Johnstone B. M, Cook-Newell M. E. Meta-analysis of the effects of soy protein intake on serum lipids. New England Journal of Medicine. 1995;333:276-282. (PubMed).

Arjmandi B. H, Khalil D. A, Smith B. J, Lucas E. A, Juma S, Payton M. E, Wild R. A. Soy protein has a greater effect on bone in postmenopausal women not on hormone replacement therapy, as evidenced by reducing bone resorption and urinary calcium excretion. Journal of Clinical Endocrinology & Metabolism. 2003;88:1048-1054. (PubMed).

Arliss R. M, Biermann C. A. Do soy isoflavones lower cholesterol, inhibit atherosclerosis, and play a role in cancer prevention? Holistic Nurse Practitioner. 2002;16(5):40-48. (PubMed).

Bhathena S. J, Velasquez M. T. Beneficial role of dietary phytoestrogens in obesity and diabetes. American Journal of Clinical Nutrition. 2002;76:1191-1201. (PubMed).

Consumers Union. 2004. Soy: Cutting through the confusion. Consumer Reports 69(7):28-31.

Dunn, A. 2000. Incorporating soy protein into a low-fat, low-cholesterol diet. Cleveland Clinic Journal of Medicine 67:767-72.

Friedman, M., and Brandon, D. 2001. Nutritional and health benefits of soy protein. Journal of Agricultural and Food Chemistry 49:1069-86.

Gu C.M., Pan H.B., Sun Z.W., Qin G.X. Effect of soybean variety on anti-nutritional factors content, and growth performance and nutrients metabolism in rat. Int. J. Mol. Sci. 2010;11:1048–1056.

Hasler CM. Position of the American Dietetic Association. Functional foods. J Am Diet Assoc. 2004; 104(5): 814-26.

Hasler C. M. The cardiovascular effects of soy products. Cardiovascular Nursing. 2002;16(4):50-63. (PubMed).

Keinan-Boker L, Peeters P. H, Mulligan A. A, Navarro C, Slimani N, Mattisson I, Lundin E, McTaggart A, Allen N. E, Overvad K, Tjonneland A, Clavel-Chapelon F, Linseisen J, Haftenberger M, Lagiou P, Kalapothaki V, Evangelista A, Frasca G, Bueno-deMesquita H. B, vaqn der Schouw Y. T, Engeset D, Skeie G, Tormo M. J, Ardanaz E, Charrodiere U. R, Riboli E. Soy product consumption in 10 European countries: The European Prospective Investigation into Cancer and Nutrition (EPIC) study. Public Health Nutrition. 2002;5(6B):1217-1226. (PubMed).

Liener, I.E., 1994. Implication of anti-nutritional components in soybeans foods. Crit. Rev. Food Sci. Nutr., 34: 31-67.

Munro I. C, Harwood M, Hlywka J. J, Stephe A. M, Doull J, Flamm W. G, Adlerereutz H. Soy isoflavones: A safety review. Nutrition Review. 2003;61:1-33. (PubMed).

Nedrow A, et al. Complementary and alternative therapies for the management of menopause-related symptoms: a systematic evidence review. Arch Intern Med. 2006 Jul 24; 166(14): 1453-65.

Peeters, P., et al. 2003. Phytoestrogens and breast cancer risk. Review of the epidemiological evidence. Breast Cancer Research and Treatment 77:171-83.

Sacks FM, Lichtenstein A, Van Horn L, Harris W, Kris-Etherton P, Winston M. Soy protein, isoflavones, and cardiovascular health: an American Heart Association Science Advisory for professionals from the Nutrition Committee. Circulation. 2006 Feb 21; 113(7): 1034-44. Epub 2006 Jan 17.

Whitney E. N, Rolfes S. R. 2002. Understanding nutrition (9th ed.). Belmont, CA: Wadsworth.

CHAPTER 7
WHEAT PROTEIN

INTRODUCTION

This book has reiterated the health benefits that support a dietary shift towards plant protein, with a sparing of animal protein intake. This shift has many associated merits including both ecological and health benefits. Health benefits of plant protein rich diets involve the promotion of cardiovascular health, weight control, cancer prevention and improvements in bone health. The anticipated rise in the world population has created a need to examine sustainable sources such as plant proteins to replace inefficient sources of animal protein.

Table 22 shows examples of grains with substantial protein to carbohydrate ratios. Unrefined whole grains tend to provide more protein content per carbohydrate content.

PROTEIN TO CARBOHYDRATE RATIO	GRAIN
1 gram protein to 2.5 grams of carbs	Wheat
1 gram of protein to 3 grams of carbs	Oat Bran
1 gram of protein to 4 grams of carbs	Rice Bran Oats Wheat Bran Japanese Soba Noodles
1 gram of protein to 4.5 grams of carbs	Hard Red Spring Wheat Quinoa Amaranth
1 gram of protein to 5 grams of carbs	Kamut Rye Spelt Whole-Wheat Macaroni Wild Rice Teff Durum Wheat Whole-Grain Wheat Flour Buckwheat

1 gram of protein to 6 grams of carbs	Triticale Hard Red Winter Wheat Semolina Barley Bulgur Couscous
1 gram of protein to 7 grams of carbs	Japanese Somen Noodles Sorghum Millet Hard White Wheat Chinese Chow Mein Noodles
1 gram of protein to 8 grams of carbs	Yellow Corn White Corn
1 gram of protein to 9 grams of carbs	Brown Rice

Table 22. Examples of grains with high protein to carbohydrate content ratios.

WHEAT PROTEIN

Wheat and its associated protein is ubiquitous in the human food chain. Table 23 provides a list of examples of common foods that contain wheat protein and those that often have a wheat content.

WHEAT PROTEIN PRESENT	WHEAT PROTEIN OFTEN PRESENT
Bran	Acker meal
Bread crumbs	Ale and beer
Bulgur	Baking mixes
Couscous	Baked goods, including cookies
Durum, durum flour, and durum wheat	Breaded and batter-fried foods
Einkorn	Cereals
Farina	Hot dogs and processed meats
Farro (also known as emmer)	Ice cream
Kamut	Salad dressing
Semolina	Pasta
Sprouted wheat	Sauces and soups
Triticale	Soy sauce
Wheat (bran, germ, gluten, grass, malt, starch)	Surimi (mock crab meat)

Wheat berries	
Wheat flour (all types, including all-purpose)	

Table 23. Foods that have wheat content and foods in which wheat is often present (source WebMD: www.webmd.com/allergies/guide/wheat-allergy).

Wheat has been a part of the food chain for thousands of years and its domesticated origin can be traced to the near Middle East about 11,000 years ago. Types of wheat have been classified in many ways such as planting season varieties, hardness of grain and botanical origin. Wheat has evolved with many genetic variants produced by cross breeding practices among cereal grains. While genetic modification of wheat has not been extensively used, the production of this form of wheat will undoubtedly increase in the next few years.

Soft types of wheat contain much starch and have less gluten content than "hard" wheat. Hard wheat is ideally suited for the making of flour, bread and cakes because of its higher gluten and protein content. In contrast, soft wheat is preferred for the production of biscuits, breakfast foods and French bread. One working classification of different types of wheat is shown below in Table 24.

TYPE OF WHEAT	COMMENTS
HARD VARIETIES:	
Hard Red Winter	Use in bread and all purpose flour, about 40% of U.S. crop
Durum Wheat	High protein and high gluten used in pasta and semolina flour
Hard Red Spring	High protein used in bread, baking and flour blends
Hard White Wheat	Medium protein grain used in hard rolls, bulgar, tortillas, oriental noodles and brewing
SOFT VARIETIES:	
Soft Red Winter	Low to medium protein content used in a blended

	form in cookies, cakes and donuts
Soft White Wheat	Low protein wheat used in crackers, pastries, Asian style noodles, flatbreads and cakes

Table 24: A working classification of different types of wheat.

While most cereals are preponderant in their contents of carbohydrates, wheat, rice and maize contain a substantial range of (protein content 7-12% protein). The principal amino acids that form cereal proteins are glutamine, proline and glycine. As noted earlier, cereal proteins of different types include: albumins, globulins, glutelins and prolamins.

Globulin-type proteins are soluble in salt solutions and albumin is soluble in water. These two types of protein have major differences in their distribution in plant proteins. For example, globulins are present in amounts of 3% in maize and 55% in oats. Prolamins are classified as sulphur rich, sulphur poor and high molecular weight types. These complex mixtures of prolamins can also be classified by their solubility characteristics into: hordeins, secalins and gliadins.

Glutelins are proteins associated with gliadins that form the gluten molecule. Gluten is a protein associated with the causation of celiac disease or gluten enteropathy and it is found in rye, barley and wheat. While gliadin is the main potentially toxic protein contained in wheat, glutelins are also present in rice (oryzenin), but they are not associated with gluten enteropathy (celiac disease, or dermatitis herpetiformis). That said, there are other proteins perhaps related to gluten that can cause wheat allergy which is a disorder that is quite different than celiac disease.

PROPERTIES OF WHEAT PROTEIN

An excellent overview of wheat science is present in the book entitled "Wheat Chemistry and Technology" (edited by Khan K. and Shewry, P., 2009, ISBN, 978-1-891127-55-7). In this latter book, the relationship between the structure and functional properties of wheat protein is reviewed with an extensive discussion of transgenic manipulation of wheat qualities. In brief, it has been long recognized that the nutritional and functional qualities of wheat are related to the amino acid composition of its protein (Krull, H., Wall, J.S., Bakers Digest, 1969, 43, 4, 30-34).

Gluten protein accounts for about 80% of wheat flour proteins and albumins together with globulins, which compose the remaining 20%. Gluten protein is found as gliadin and glutenin, which differ in physico-chemical properties when hydrated. Hydration renders gliadin into a thick fluid and glutenin confers visco-elastic and cohesive properties. These latter qualities are extremely important in producing high quality baked goods.

Wheat protein contains 21 different amino acids that form polypeptide structures with many different sequences. Gluten proteins have a relatively low concentration of ionizable amino acids in comparison with albumin and globulins, which are soluble in aqueous media. The most prevalent group of amino acids in wheat gluten (gliadin and glutenin) are non-polar including: alanine, valine, glycine, isoleucine, phenylalanine and proline. These amino acids account for up to 50% of residues found in wheat proteins.

In summary, the properties of the various wheat proteins are related to amino acid composition. A prized property of wheat protein is related to its cohesive properties. These properties are due to functional groups of the various amino-acid building blocks of the protein. These groups can form hydrophobic and hydrogen bonds which determine cohesion when multiplied together. In the case of gluten, disulphide bonding forms between polypeptide chains, thereby enhancing visco-elastic properties.

Gluten is a common food stuff, with particular popularity in Asian cuisine. Wheat gluten enjoys similar uses as soybean solid meat substitutes such as tofu. It is sometimes referred to as wheat meat or as seitan in Japan. Gluten is found in the hydrolyzed form by treatment with acid. The hydrolyzed form of gluten is composed of a mixture of smaller size protein fragments, polypeptides and amino acids that is easier to digest than gluten. This form of wheat protein is a flavor enhancer due to its significant content of glutamate that activates specialized tongue receptors that sense savory flavors. It has been suggested that fully hydrolyzed protein is gluten free, but its composition must be avoided in the presence of gluten enteropathy.

The manufacture of wheat flour leaves a residue that is high in protein content, called wheat protein isolate. This isolate is about 85% protein and it is very useful in baking because of its ability to improve mouth feel, texture and softness.

GLUTEN ENTEROPATHY (CELIAC DISEASE)

Celiac disease is an example of gluten intolerance that causes immunological changes of delayed hypersensitivity. It is not mediated by allergen specific antibodies, including IgE. Gluten is a component of a number of grains, most notably wheat, rye and barley. Some doubt has been cast on oats as a source of gluten, but the presence of gluten in oats can be due to common cross contamination among grains (e.g. during storage). The whole subject of wheat allergy or intolerance has been complicated by new definitions of gluten intolerance in the absence of criteria that are necessary to support the diagnosis of celiac disease (non-celiac-gluten-sensitivity).

The complexity of gluten intolerance and the separate status of wheat allergy have led to a series of descriptions of disorders, under the overall umbrella of the Oslo Definition(s) (Ludvigsson, J.F. et al Gut online February 16, 2012, doi: 10:A136/gutin1-2011-301346). Terminology related to gluten intolerance has been made confusing because the use of names of the subtypes of the disorders: notably celiac disease (CD), asymptomatic CD, potential CD, subclinical CD, symptomatic CD, non-celiac gluten sensitivity and a separate description of gluten-sensitivity related disorders, such as dermatitis herpetiformis and gluten-ataxia.

In brief, celiac disease results in a cell-mediated inflammation of the gut with flattening of the villi of the small intestines (subtotal villous atrophy). These intestinal lesions alter the absorptive and secretory capacity of the small bowel. Along with enhancement of intestinal permeability, malabsorption of food occurs and net fluid loss may occur in the small intestine. There appears to be a defect in mucosal handling of gliadin with the generation of toxic peptides that provoke a delayed hypersensitivity phenomenon.

Celiac disease presents with a wide spectrum of symptoms and signs in both children and adults. Malabsorption syndrome may be associated with wasting, general gastrointestinal upset, diarrhea and abdominal bloating. Systemic symptoms and signs are common with weakness, signs of anemia and bone pain. A wide variety of nutritional deficiencies and their consequences may be present in the individual with overt celiac disease.

The causative agent in celiac disease is found in the gluten protein fractions of wheat, rye and barley. Celiac disease is a persistent illness that is only responsive to prolonged and careful withdrawal of gluten from the diet. The prevalence of celiac disease has been estimated to be as common as 1 in 133 of the population if one takes accounts of serological testing for the disorder (e.g. anti-endomysial antibody or tissue transglutaminase antibody). Using diagnostic small intestinal mucosal biopsies, the occurrence of celiac disease is less common. There is no doubt that accurate estimates of the prevalence of celiac disease are increased by the intensity of diagnostic testing.

The prevalence of latent or silent celiac disease remains unclear. Some of these individuals may react positively for anti-endomysial antibodies, but they may not show any adverse effects to gluten challenge or the presence of gluten in the diet. It is generally accepted that the presence of celiac disease is higher in European countries and Australia in comparison with the U.S., but the differences of prevalence may be due in part to the application of different types of diagnostic testing.

Gluten enteropathy is a life-long disorder and tolerance to gluten does not develop in the long term. Most people with celiac disease have to avoid wheat, rye and barley, but, as mentioned earlier, they should also avoid oats because of cross contamination among grains. The increasing demand for gluten free foods has driven market expansion of gluten free products. However, many gluten free products are used by individuals without celiac disease, who assume that benefits of the removal of gluten intake will occur. Many gluten-free choices of food by general consumers are probably unnecessary.

There are increasing numbers of newly detected individuals with the more recently recognized entity of non-celiac gluten intolerance. Some of these individuals have the common condition of wheat allergy which is antibody mediated wheat intolerance. Wheat allergy is a distinct disorder not involving the delayed hypersensitivity reactions that are found in celiac disease. The smallest dosages of wheat, barley and rye that may elicit celiac disease are estimated to be approximately 10 mg of gliadin per day. The Codex Alimentarius Commission has defined gluten free foods as containing less that 20 ppm (parts per million) of gluten and this level has been accepted in many countries, but not in the U.S. It is important to recognize ingredients that are specifically derived from gluten. (Table 25).

Soy Sauce	Caramel
Gluten	Malt/malt extract
Hydrolyzed wheat protein	B-Glucan
Wheat bran hydrolysate	Alcohol/ethanol
Wheat protein isolate	Vinegar
Wheat bran	Wheat germ oil?
Wheat starch	Xanthan gum
Wheat starch hydrolysate	Bacterial culture
Wheat maltodextrin	Yeast
Sorbitol, lactitol, maltitol	Enzymes

Table 25. Food ingredients that contain gluten.

Wheat allergy can occur by ingestion of wheat or skin contact. The immunological basis of this disorder involves mast cell responses and immunoglobulin E (IgE) production. More than two dozen wheat allergens have been identified, but many more are believed to exist. Wheat allergy is uncommon and it is most often due to allergic responses to prolamin and glutelins, but more severe responses occur with gliadin. All of the protein components of wheat that cause allergies have not been isolated but they include globulin or albumin derivatives, amylase/trypsin inhibitors (serpins) and lipid transfer proteins.

Wheat allergies share much in common with other antibody-mediated food allergies. Symptoms and signs of wheat allergies include eczema, sacro-ileitis, hives, hay fever, asthma and gastrointestinal upset. Frequent associations with wheat allergy include: urticaria and exercise/aspirin induced anaphylaxis. Wheat allergy has been proposed to be an underlying factor in the development of recurrent migraine, inflammatory arthropathy and autism, but variable evidence exists. A number of new studies suggest that gluten sensitivity may be confused with a range of disorders that are triggered by many different allergens found in wheat and other grains.

WHEAT: GENERAL INFORMATION

Wheat has complicated cultivation origins from repeated harvesting and sowing of grains or grasses. Farming practices have resulted in the selection of several mutant forms of wheat of large grain size. The genetics of wheat cultivation are highly complex with: enkorn wheat (Triticum monococcum), a diploid (two sets of chromosomes), tetraploid wheats (called emmer and durum) and hexaploid wheat (spelt wheat and bread wheat). The major objectives of wheat breeding have been to develop wheat resistance to thermal influences, high nutritional content, insect resistance and tolerance to abiotic stressors.

There are many different botanical classification systems for wheat and the taxonomy of wheat can be quite confusing. As mentioned earlier, other ways of classifying different species of wheat include: protein contents, growing season, quality of the contents of gluten (strong or elastic properties) and grain color. Raw wheat is often ground into flour, germinated and dried to produce malt, crushed into "cracked" wheat or parboiled and further processed into bulgur (groats). Wheat is a main ingredient in many different foods including: pastries, cookies, pies, pancakes, break, porridge, crackers, muesli and a wide range of breakfast cereals and baked goods.

While wheat starch is a prominent product of wheat, it is not as economically significant as gluten content and quality. Clearly, there is much variation in the nutritional profile of different types of wheat and these differences are apparent at seasonal growing times, e.g. spring versus winter. For example, hard red wheat grown in the winter has usually about 12.6 grams of protein per 100 grams (3.5 oz), whereas hard red spring wheat has more protein of about 15.4 grams of protein per 100 gram. Table 26 shows the average amounts of macro and micronutrients contained in hard red winter wheat.

NUTRITIONAL VALUE PER 100G (3.5 OZ)	
Energy	1,368 Kj (327 kcal)
Carbohydrates	71.18 g
-Sugars	0.41
-Dietary fiber	12.2 g
Fat	1.54 g
Protein	12.61 g
Thiamine (vit. B_1)	0.383 mg (33%)
Riboflavin (vit. B_2)	0.115 mg (10%)
Niacin (vit. B_3)	5.464 mg (36%)
Pantothenic acid (B_5)	0.954 mg (19%)
Vitamin B_6	0.3 mg (23%)
Folate (vit. B_9)	38 ug (10%)
Vitamin E	1.01 mg (7%)
Vitamin K	1.9 ug (2%)
Calcium	29 mg (3%)
Iron	3.19 mg (25%)
Magnesium	126 mg (35%)
Manganese	3.985 mg (190%)
Phosphorus	288 mg (41%)
Potassium	363 mg (8%)
Sodium	2 mg (0%)
Zinc	2.65 mg (28%)

Table 26. Nutritional contents of wheat, hard red winter.

Wheat is a common source of carbohydrates and protein for the world population. Wheat protein is readily digested by 98% of individuals but the occurrence of gluten intolerance and wheat allergy, real or misdiagnosed, are causing an increasing switch to other forms of protein.

WHEAT, DISEASE AND OBESITY

In the controversial book entitled "Wheat Belly," Dr. William Davis espouses a number of opinions about wheat as a common source of illness and disease. In this book, it is argued that wheat is the single largest contributor to the nation's obesity epidemic and a wide range of other disorders including: skin diseases, cancer, diabetes, digestive disorders, cardiovascular disease, dementia and general body aging.

Some of the opinions expressed by Dr. Davis have been challenged, especially by credible sources such as the National Wheat Improvement Committee (NWIC). In brief, the NWIC corrects some of the misunderstandings propagated by Dr. Davis and his supporters. This "Davis group" proposes that genetic modification (GMO) of wheat is responsible for the emergence of more celiac disease and wheat-related disorders. The NWIC stress that gene transfer (classic GMO technology) is not an issue, at present, with wheat. New varieties of wheat are usually bred by conventional crossing of genes that combine to form new genetic combinations, not gene transfer (to produce GMO). While other methods of "crossing" exist, they are generally not "classic" GMO gene transfers.

Novel ideas about wheat derivatives crossing the blood brain barrier and stimulating appetite have been proposed by Dr. Davis, but the evidence for such circumstances is lacking. Dr. Davis has described modern wheat as a "perfect, chronic poison" and he believes that its content of gliadin bears some similarity to the actions of opiates (Cochrane, A., CBS News, June 21, 2013). In a news interview (Cochrane, A., ibid, 2013), Dr. Davis predicted that over 90% of all grains eaten in the U.S. in future years will be of wheat origin. Furthermore, he is convinced that wheat exclusion from the diet would reduce the prevalence of diabetes mellitus, arthritis, acid reflux, irritable bowel syndrome and depression. Clearly, polar differences of opinion exist on these issues and health advisors often recommend wheat as a valuable component of a balanced diet.

The gluten free market is growing rapidly with projected increases from 4.2 billion dollars in 2012 to 6.6 billion dollars in 2017. While gluten is the culprit in the causation of celiac disease, it has been speculated that modern wheat is capable of producing thousands of different proteins, each of which is theoretically capable of promoting an inflammatory response or allergic properties that differ from the delayed hypersensitivity reactions that occur in gluten enteropathy (celiac disease).

WHEAT GERM AGGLUTININ

Wheat germ agglutinin (WGA) is an example of a lectin. Lectins are compounds that selectively bind to certain proteins and they are widespread in life forms. A protein known as N-Acetylglucosamine (NAG) is found on the surfaces of insects, fungi and bacteria. This compound is also a key component of several body tissues, such as tendons, articular surfaces of joints, cartilaginous tissues and the lining of blood vessels and the digestive tract. N-Acetylglucosamine reacts with WGA and it causes tissue damage. The presence of NAG and its reactivity with WGA is believed to be responsible for many negative effects of wheat that are vague and difficult to diagnose.

It is known that WGA can cause direct damage to many tissues in the human body. This damage can occur without involving complex immune mechanisms and it may occur without the presence of any genetic susceptibility. These circumstances assist in understanding why chronic inflammatory disorders are sometimes found in populations who consume wheat, in the absence of overt signs of wheat intolerance. While much further research is required on these issues, non-gluten-induced wheat disorders are of increasing concern.

SEITAN

Seitan is made from gluten and is referred to as wheat meat. In Japan, it is known as "kofu". It serves a function of making bread dough more elastic but it is most often consumed as textured meat substitute that is high in protein, low in fat and firm in its consistency. Seitan contains per weight more plant protein than tofu and it contains B vitamins and iron. Moreover, it contains no saturated fat or cholesterol, but it is often high in sodium content (sometimes salt is added).

Seitan is useful as a staple in vegetarian diets along with tofu and tempeh which are made from soybeans. Table 27 shows the general nutritional content of these forms of plant protein.

3 oz serving	Firm tofu	Tempeh	Seitan
Calories	70	173	90
Fat (g)	3.5	6	1
Sodium (mg)	20	8	380
Carbs (g)	2	12	3
Fiber (g)	<1	9	1
Protein (g)	8	16.6	18

Table 27. Nutritional Values of tofu, tempeh and seitan.

Tofu, Tempeh and Seitan have several distinct flavors and ways of cooking: Seitan ("wheat meat", "mock duck") is an option to limit soy intake while on a vegetarian diet. It's origin from gluten makes it contraindicated in patients with celiac disease, dermatitis herpeteformis and gluten sensitivity. It has a consistency and appearance similar to meat. Tofu is smooth white soybean-derived material with a spongy consistency that may be presented in a firm or very soft manner. It has a mild taste that when cooked is capable of absorbing the flavor of mixed foods. Tempeh is a light brown textured soy product that is made by fermenting cooked soybeans. It is presented in square or rectangular blocks and it has a nutty flavor such that it can be eaten raw or cooked in a variety of ways.

CONCLUSION

Wheat is a common dietary staple. It presents many possibilities of allergic or food intolerance responses. Wheat allergies should not be confused with gluten sensitivity or gluten enteropathy (celiac disease).

WHEAT REFERENCES

Akagawa M, Handoyo T, Ishii T, Kumazawa S, Morita N, Suyama K (2007). Proteomic analysis of wheat flour allergens. *J. Agric. Food Chem.* 55 (17): 6863–70. doi:10.1021/jf070843a.

Akiyama H; Sakata K; Yoshioka Y et al. (2006). Profile analysis and immunoglobulin E reactivity of wheat protein hydrolysates. *Int. Arch. Allergy Immunol.* 140 (1): 36–42. Doi:10.1159/000092000.

Allport, Susan. The Queen of Fats: Why Omega-3s Were Removed from the Western Diet and What We Can Do to Replace Them (Berkeley: University of California Press, 2006).

Ames, Bruce N. Increasing Longevity by Tuning Up Metabolism. European Molecular Biology Organization. 6 (2005): S20-S24.

Andrich DE, Filion ME, Woods M, Dwyer JT, Gorbach SL, Goldin BR, Adlercreutz H, Aubertin-Leheudre M. Relationship between essential amino acids and muscle mass, independent of habitual diets, in pre- and post-menopausal US women. Int J Food Sci Nutr. 2011 Nov;62(7):719-24. Epub 2011 May 16.

Armentia A, Sanchez-Monge R, Gomez L, Barber D, Salcedo G (1993). "*In vivo* allergenic activities of eleven purified members of a major allergen family from wheat and barley flour". *Clin. Exp. Allergy* 23 (5): 410–5. Doi:10.1111/j.1365-2222.1993.tb00347.x

Baldo BA, Krilis S, Wrigley CW (1980). Hypersensitivity to inhaled flour allergens. Comparison between cereals. *Allergy* 35 (1): 45–56. doi: 10.1111/j.1398-9995.1980.tb01716.x

Barnetson RS, Wright AL, Benton EC (1989). IgE-mediated allergy in adults with severe atopic eczema. *Clin. Exp. Allergy* 19 (3): 321–5. doi:10.1111/j.1365-2222.1989.tb02390.x.

Blands J, Diamant B, Kallós P, Kallós-Deffner L, Lowenstein H (1976). Flour allergy in bakers. I. Identification of allergenic fractions in flour and comparison of diagnostic methods. *Int. Arch. Allergy Appl. Immunol.* 52 (1–4): 392–406.

Campbell, T. Colin. Letters to the Editor: Animal Protein and Ischemic Heart Disease. American Journal of Clinical Nutrition. 71.3 (2000): 849-50.

Campbell, T. Colin, and Thomas M. Campbell II. The China Study (Dallas: BenBella Books, Inc., 2006).

Caso G, Scalfi L, Marra M, Covino A, Muscaritoli M, McNurlan MA, Garlick PJ, Contaldo F. Albumin synthesis is diminished in men consuming a predominantly vegetarian diet. J Nutr. 2000 Mar;130(3):528-33.

De Lorgeril, Michel. Mediterranean Diet, Traditional Risk Factors, and the Rate of Cardiovascular Complications After Myocardial Infarction: Final Report of the Lyon Diet Heart Study. Journal of the American Heart Association. 99 (1999): 779-85.

Diamond, Jared. Guns, Germs, and Steel (New York: W. W. Norton & Company, 1999).

Dietary Reference Intakes: Macronutrients. National Academy of Sciences. Institute of Medicine. Food and Nutrition Board. DRI table for carbohydrate, fiber, fat, fatty acids and protein.

Dieterich W, Esslinger B, Trapp D, Hahn E, Huff T, Seilmeier W, Wieser H, and Schuppan D. (2006). Cross linking to tissue transglutaminase and collagen favours gliadin toxicity in coeliac disease. *Gut.* **55** (4): 478–84. doi:10.1136/gut.2005.069385.

Donovan GR, Baldo BA (1990). Crossreactivity of IgE antibodies from sera of subjects allergic to both ryegrass pollen and wheat endosperm proteins: evidence for common allergenic determinants. *Clin. Exp. Allergy* 20 (5): 501–9. Doi:10.1111/j.1365-2222.1990.tb03142.x

Doyle MD, Morse LM, Gowan JS, Parsons MR. Observations on nitrogen and energy balance in young men consuming vegetarian diets. Am J Clin Nutr. 1965 Dec;17(6):367-76.

Elango R, Humayun MA, Ball RO, Pencharz PB. Evidence that protein requirements have been significantly underestimated. Curr Opin Clin Nutr Metab Care. 2010 Jan;13(1):52-7.

Ford, Earl S., et al. Explaining the Decrease in U.S. Deaths from Coronary Disease. 1980-2000. New England Journal of Medicine. 356.23 (2007): 2388-98.

Freudenheim, Jo L. Study Design and Hypothesis Testing: Issues in the Evaluation of Evidence from Research in Nutritional Epidemiology. American Journal of Clinical Nutrition. 69 (1999): 1315S-21S.

Gaffney-Stomberg E, Insogna KL, Rodriguez NR, Kerstetter JE. Increasing dietary protein requirements in elderly people for optimal muscle and bone health. J Am Geriatr Soc. 2009 Jun;57(6):1073-9.

Grant EC (1979). Food allergies and migraine. *Lancet* **1** (8123): 966–9. doi:10.1016/S0140-6736(79).

Gregg, Edward W., et al. Trends in the Prevalence and Ratio of Diagnosed to Undiagnosed Diabetes According to Obesity Levels in the U.S. Diabetes Care. 27(2004): 2806-12.

Haddad EH, Berk LS, Kettering JD, Hubbard RW, Peters WR. Dietary intake and biochemical, hematologic, and immune status of vegans compared with nonvegetarians. Am J Clin Nutr. 1999 Sep;70(3 Suppl):586S-593S.

Haslam, David W., and W. Philip T. James. Obesity. The Lancet. 336 (2005): 1197-1209.

Key, Timothy J., et al. Diet, Nutrition and the Prevention of Cancer. Public Health Nutrition. 7.1A (2004): 187-200.

Kris-Etherton, P.M., et al. Polyunsaturated Fatty Acids in the Food Chain in the United States. American Journal of Clinical Nutrition. 71 (2000): 179S-88S.

Laurière M; Pecquet C; Bouchez-Mahiout I et al. (2006). Hydrolysed wheat proteins present in cosmetics can induce immediate hypersensitivities. *Contact Derm.* 54 (5): 283–9. Doi:10.1111/j.0105-1873.2006.00830.x

Liu, Simin, et al. Fruit and Vegetable Intake and Risk of Cardiovascular Disease: The Women's Health Study. American Journal of Clinical Nutrition. 72 (2000): 922-28.

Melton, Lisa. The Antioxidant Myth. New Scientist (August 5-11, 2006).

Morais JA, Chevalier S, Gougeon R. Protein turnover and requirements in the healthy and frail elderly. J Nutr Health Aging. 2006 Jul-Aug;10(4):272-83.

Morita E, Kunie K, Matsuo H (2007). Food-dependent exercise-induced anaphylaxis. *J. Dermatol. Sci.* 47 (2): 109–17. doi:10.1016/j.jdermsci.2007.03.004.

Narayan, K. M. Venkat, et al. Lifetime Risk for Diabetes Mellitus in the United States. Journal of the American Medical Association. 290.14 (2003): 1884-90.

National Research Council. Diet, Nutrition and Cancer (Washington, D.C.: National Academy Press, 1982).

Nestle, Marion. Food Politics (Berkeley: University of California Press, 2002).

Nutritional Health: Strategies for Disease Prevention. Edited by Ted Wilson and Norman J. Temple (Totowa, NJ: Humana Press, INC., 2001).

Paddon-Jones D, Short KR, Campbell WW, Volpi E, Wolfe RR. Role of dietary protein in the sarcopenia of aging. Am J Clin Nutr. 2008 May;87(5):1562S-1566S.

Pastorello EA; Farioli L; Conti A et al. (2007). Wheat IgE-mediated food allergy in European patients: alpha-amylase inhibitors, lipid transfer proteins and low-molecular-weight glutenins. Allergenic molecules recognized by double-blind, placebo-controlled food challenge. *Int. Arch. Allergy Immunol.* 144 (1): 10–22. Doi:101159/000102609.

Perr HA (2006). Novel foods to treat food allergy and gastrointestinal infection. *Current allergy and asthma reports* 6 (2): 153–9. doi: 10.1007/s11882-006-0054-z.

Planck, Nina. Real Food: What to Eat and Why (New York: Bloomsbury, 2006).

Pollan, Michael. The Omnivore's Dilemma (New York: The Penguin Press, 2006).

Position of the American Dietetic Association, Dietitians of Canada, and the American College of Sports Medicine: Nutrition and Athletic Performance. J Am Diet Assoc. 2009;109:509-527.

Price, Weston A. Nutrition and Physical Degeneration, 7th edition (LaMesa: Price-Pottenger Nutrition Foundation, Inc., 2006).

Rand WM, Pellett PL, Young VR. Meta-analysis of nitrogen balance studies for estimating protein requirements in healthy adults. Am J Clin Nutr. 2003 Jan;77(1):109-27.

Register UD, Inano M, Thurston CE, Vyhmeister IB, Dysinger PW, Blankenship JW, Horning MC. Nitrogen-balance studies in human subjects on various diets. Am J Clin Nutr. 1967 Jul;20(7):753-9.

Rosamond, Wayne D., et al. Trends in the incidence of Myocardial Infarction and in Mortality Due to Coronary Heart Disease, 1987 to 1994. New England Journal of Medicine. 339.13 (1998): 861-67.

Rozin, Paul. Human Food Intake and Choice: Biological, Psychological and Cultural Perspectives. (Philadelphia: University of Pennsylvania, 2002). Available online at http://www.danone-institute.com/publications/ book/pdf/food_selection_01_rozin.pdf.

Rubio-Tapia A, Murray J. Gluten-sensitive enteropathy. In: Metcalfe DD, Sampson HA, Simon RA, eds. Food Allergy – Adverse Reactions to Foods and Food Additives. 4th ed. Malden MA: Blackwell Science. 2008:211-22.

Sotkovský P, Sklenář J, Halada P, Cinová J, Setinová I, Kainarová A, Goliáš J, Pavlásková K, Honzová S, Tučková L., A new approach to the isolation and characterization of wheat flour allergens., *Clin Exp Allergy.* 2011 Jul;41(7):1031-43

Sutton R, Hill DJ, Baldo BA, Wrigley CW (1982). Immunoglobulin E antibodies to ingested cereal flour components: studies with sera from subjects with asthma and eczema. *Clin. Allergy* 12 (1): 63–74. doi:10.1111/j.1365-2222.1982.tb03127.x

Temple, Norman J., and Denis P. Burkitt. Western Diseases (New Jersey: Humana Press Inc., 1994).

Trichopoulou, A., and E. Vasilopoulou. Mediterranean Diet and Longevity. British Journal of Nutrition. 84 suppl. 2 (2000): S205-59.

Walsh BJ, Wrigley CW, Musk AW, Baldo BA (1985). A comparison of the binding of IgE in the sera of patients with bakers' asthma to soluble and insoluble wheat-grain proteins. *J. Allergy Clin. Immunol.* 76 (1): 23–8. Doi: 10.1016/0091-6749(85)90799-7.

Weichel M, Glaser AG, Ballmer-Weber BK, Schmid-Grendelmeier P, Crameri R (2006). Wheat and maize thioredoxins: a novel cross-reactive cereal allergen family related to baker's asthma. *J. Allergy Clin. Immunol.* 117 (3): 676–81. Doi:10.1016/j.jaci.2005.11.040.

Western Diseases. Edited by Norman J. Temple and Denis P. Burkitt (Totowa, NJ: Humana Press Inc., 1994).

Willett, Walter C. Diet and Cancer: One View at the Start of the Millennium. Cancer Epidemiology, Biomarkers & Prevention. 10 (2001): 3-8.

Yáñez E, Uauy R, Zacarías I, Barrera G. Long-term validation of 1 g of protein per kilogram body weight from a predominantly vegetable mixed diet to meet the requirements of young adult males. J Nutr. 1986 May;116(5):865-72.

Yazicioglu M, Oner N, Celtik C, Okutan O, Pala O (2004). Sensitization to common allergens, especially pollens, among children with respiratory allergy in the Trakya region of Turkey. *Asian Pac. J. Allergy Immunol.* 22 (4): 183–90.

Zeiger RS; Heller S; Mellon MH et al. (1989). Effect of combined maternal and infant food-allergen avoidance on development of atopy in early infancy: a randomized study. *J. Allergy Clin. Immunol.* 84 (1): 72–89. doi:10.1016/0091-6749(89)90181-4.

CHAPTER 8

OTHER PROTEINS

There are many different types of plant protein that have gained popularity but some are misclassified. For example, protein sources with valuable biological properties including spirulina and mycoproteins are not plant proteins per se. In this chapter a number of "other proteins" are discussed in variable detail. On occasion the proteins discussed in this section of the book are sometimes referred to as "designer proteins" Table 28.

TYPES OF PROTEIN (DESIGNER PROTEINS)

- Lupin
- Chia
- Spirulina
- Quinoa
- Nut protein
- Edamame
- Mycoprotein (Quorn)
- Seitan
- Various seeds, e.g. sunflower, sesame, Chia, hemp, flax, and pumpkin seeds.
- Canola
- Corn
- Lentils
- Nutritional yeast
- Beans
- Buck wheat
- Ezekial bread
- Hummus

Table 28. Examples of plant proteins that have become increasingly popular inclusions in designer or functional foods and dietary supplements. Please note that "plant proteins" are terms applied loosely to several dietary sources of protein.

LUPIN PROTEIN

In recent years, attention has been focused on the use of lupin protein in human nutrition. Lupin presents a good source of amino acids. Lupin protein differs from soy protein by its low content of isoflavones and antinutritional factors, e.g., phytate, tannins, lectins, protease inhibitors and undigestible oligosaccharides.

Lupin is a common plant name for several domestic species which include Lupin albus (white lupin), L. luteus (yellow lupin), L. mutabilis (blue lupin), and L. angustifolius (narrow leaf lupin). Lupins are cultivated often in Australia, Russia, France, and other European countries. Proteins derived from white lupin and blue lupin have been well documented to effectively alter blood lipoprotein profiles and blood pressure in a favorable manner. Furthermore, studies in patients with hypercholesterolemia have demonstrated that lupin proteins may cause a reduction in circulating levels of C-reactive protein (hs-CRP, a marker of inflammation).

Lupin proteins have been studied quite extensively as animal feed and they contain two major types of protein (albumin and globulin components). Studies of lupin seed meals in rats show a significant reduction of hypercholesterolemia. Sirtori et al (Sirtori, C.R.; Lovati, M.R.; Manzoni, C.; Castiglioni, S.; Duranti, M.; Magni, C.; Morandi, S.; D'Agostina, A.; and Arnoldi, A.; J. Nutr., Jan., 2004, vol 134, 8-23). In these studies, white lupin seeds were the source of lupin, which was gavaged for two weeks in rats who received a casein-based cholesterol and cholic acid diet. The lupin protein extract reduced total plasma cholesterol and VLDL and LDL by significant amounts (21% and 30%, respectively). Studies of LDL receptor activity in these experiments showed stimulation of these receptors by certain protein components of the lupin. This upregulation of the LDL receptor is a well defined mechanism of blood cholesterol reduction by vegetable or plant proteins.

Studies in human volunteers show that lupin protein has a beneficial effect on plasma LDL and LDL:HDL cholesterol ratios (Bahr, M.; Fechner, A.; Kramer, J.; Kientopf, M.; Jahreis, G.; Nutrition Journal, 2013, 12, 107). In these studies, it was found that 25 grams of lupin protein reduced plasma LDL and blood pressure over the short term. In brief, this randomized crossover study showed that 25 grams of supplemented lupin protein for four weeks can reduce total blood cholesterol (5% reduction), LDL cholesterol (12% reduction), and LDL:HDL cholesterol ratio (16% reduction). In common with many other dietary intervention studies, the effects on blood lipids were more pronounced in individuals with higher starting levels of blood cholesterol.

Some researchers have suggested that blood cholesterol lowering properties of lupin protein may be due to a low lysine:arginine ratio. The high amount of arginine in lupin protein may exert effects on blood cholesterol due to its actions on lipid-signaling molecules. Lupin protein appears to affect the expression of hepatic genes that control lipid metabolism.

Extensions of earlier observations on the lipid-lowering ability of soy protein reveals a beneficial effect of pea and lupin protein with or without the addition of soluble fiber (apple pectin or oat fiber) on lowering blood cholesterol (Sirtori, C.; Triolo, M.; Bosiso, R.; Bondioli, A.; Carabresi, L; Vergori, V.; Gomaraschi, M.; Mombelli, G.; Pazzucconi, F.; Zacherl, C.; and Arnoldi, A.; Hypocholesterolemic effects of lupin protein and pea protein/fibre combinations in moderately hypercholesterolemic individuals, British J. Nutrition, 107, 1176-1183, 2012).

CANOLA (RAPESEED PROTEIN)

Rapeseed (canola) is an important oil seed crop that can be grown at relatively low cost in many climates. It has become clear that anti-nutritive contents of several plant proteins have provided a disincentive for their use as supplemental protein sources for human nutrition. The presence of the principal anti-nutrients in rapeseed (erucic acid and glucosinolates) is reduced in canola by both selected breeding and genetic modification (e.g. the double zero type of rapeseed). Elimination of anti-nutrients from rapeseed results in a higher digestibility and bioavailability of protein components in humans (see references).

Rapeseed protein has a biological value that can meet a substantial amount of the required essential and non-essential amino acid intake. Processing techniques of rapeseed involve isolation of soluble proteins following low temperature oil extraction and/or the use of enzymatic hydrolysis to extract insoluble proteins. This can result in up to 90% recovery of protein from rapeseed in isolate form or up to an 80% yield of protein hydrolysate.

Scientific studies have confirmed efficient digestibility of canola protein in experimental animals. Furthermore, human observations demonstrate that rapeseed protein in hydrolysate and isolate form has a high nutritional quality, as measured by post-feeding blood amino acid responses. The post-prandial amino acid response to rapeseed feeding is somewhat similar to that obtained with soy protein (Fleddermann, M. et al, Nutritional evaluation of rapeseed protein compared to soy protein for quality, plasma amino acids, and nitrogen balance- A randomized cross-over intervention study in humans, Clinical Nutrition, Vol. 32, Issue 4, pp. 519-526, August 2013).

Aider, M. and Barbana, C (2011) have reviewed the composition, extraction, and application of canola proteins (rapeseed) as a food ingredient (Aider, M. Barbana, C.; Canola Proteins: Composition, extraction, functional properties, bioactivity, application as a food ingredient and allergenicity- a practical and critical review, Trends Food Sci Tech, 2011, 22, pp. 21-39). In studies by Fledderman et al (Fledderman et al, ibid, 2013), rapeseed proteins were found to be well balanced in essential amino acids in comparison to soy protein (31.9% in canola protein isolate, 37.6% in canola protein hydrolysate and 35.1% in comparative soy protein isolate, in terms of essential amino acid content). However, canola protein was found to have higher contents of sulfur-containing amino acids compared to soy protein. This difference was considered to be significant in potential biological effects of canola protein because the metabolites of sulfur rich amino acids (glutathione and homocysteine) have desirable actions as anti-oxidants.

In addition, rapeseed proteins were found to have high true digestibility scores (93.3% for canola isolate and 97.3% for canola hydrolysate) that are comparable to those found in egg, casein, and collagen (98%, 95%, and 95%, respectively) (Fledderman et al, ibid, 2013). In summary, rapeseed proteins appear to meet essential amino acid requirements in humans (Fledderman et al, ibid, 2013), but it is avoided by individuals who are against genetically modified organisms (cf soy).

CHIA PROTEIN

Chia seeds are derived from the flowering plant Salvia hispanica. Their superior nutritional profile has made these seeds a popular dietary supplement, but research studies on their functional properties remains somewhat scarce. Chia seeds contain about 30% oil, including alpha linolenic acid, ALA, with its beneficial cardiovascular and anti-inflammatory actions. Chia flour, meal and seeds are a good source of protein, fiber, anti-oxidants and several other healthy fats: 55% omega-3, 18% omega-6, 6% omega-9 and 10% saturated fat.

Chia seeds form a gel-like conglomeration when soaked in water and they are valuable additives to many foods including breakfast cereals, energy bars, smoothies and yogurt. One ounce of chia seeds delivers 157 calories in the form of 4 grams of protein and 9 grams of fat. The seeds are also mineral rich with an ounce of chia seeds containing 18% of the RDA of calcium, 27% RDA of phosphorous and 30% RDA of manganese. A summary of the nutritional profile of chia seeds is shown in table 29.

Seeds, Chia Seeds, Dried

Nutritional value per 100 g (3.5 oz)	
Energy	2,034 Kj (486 kcal)
Carbohydrates	42.12 g
-dietary fiber	34.4 g
Fat	30.74 g
-saturated	3.330
-monounsaturated	2.309
-polyunsaturated	23.665
Protein	16.54 g
Vitamin A equiv.	54 ug (7%)
Thiamine (vit. B_1)	0.62 mg (54%)
Riboflavin (vit. B_2)	0.17 mg (14%)
Niacin (vit. B_3)	8.83 mg (59%)
Folate (vit. B_9)	49 ug (12%)
Vitamin C	1.6 mg (2%)
Vitamin E	0.5 mg (3%)
Calcium	631 mg (63%)
Iron	7.72 mg (59%)
Magnesium	335 mg (94%)
Manganese	2.723 mg (130%)
Phosphorus	860 mg (123%)
Potassium	407 mg (9%)
Sodium	16 mg (1%)

| Zinc | 4.58 mg (48%) |

Table 29. Nutritional profile of dried chia seeds, USDA Nutrient Database.

In common with soybeans, hemp seed, spirulina, amaranth, quinoa and buckwheat, chia seed contains a complete protein (http://www.chialive.com.an/Chia-Complete-Protein.html). Chia seeds contain 18 of the 22 amino acids that comprise protein and it contains all 9 of the essential amino acids. However, the bioavailability of protein from chia seeds is questionable due to poor digestibility. Studies of the protein availability from Chia raw seeds, toasted seeds, toasted flour and soaked seeds indicate protein digestibility of less than 35%. Raw ground flour appears to have the highest digestibility at 78.9% (www.livestrong.com/article/490658-chia-seeds-amino-acids/).

CORN (MAIZE) PROTEIN

Corn is a grain that contains all essential amino acids in amounts that are generally low. Thus, corn is considered to be a low quality source of protein (or incomplete protein), requiring combining of other foods to meet the needs of optimal essential amino acid intake. Excessive corn intake may promote weight gain because of its high starch and associated high calorie content.

One half a cup of corn contains 80 calories and one long ear of corn contains about 100 calories. The popular habit of adding butter or margarine to corn can increase calorie load in a substantial manner. However, corn is a good source of vitamin C, B vitamins, beta-carotene and protein. Table 30 shows the nutritional profile of corn.

Fat	1.2 g
Sodium	76 mg
Potassium	347 mg
Carbohydrate	41.2 mg
Protein	5.29 g
Fiber	2.4 g
Vitamin A	11%
Vitamin C	33%
Calcium	11%

Iron	10%
Thiamin (B1)	0.045 mg
Riboflavin (B2)	0.182 mg
Niacin (B3)	2.157 mg
Vitamin B6	10.2%
Vitamin B12	0%
Magnesium	57 mg
Panthothenic Acid	0.999 mg
Zinc	5.6%
Manganese	0.091 mg

Table 30. Nutritional contents of one half a cup of corn.

SPIRULINA

Spirulina (Arthrospira spp.) is a microscopic cyanobacterium that has an ancient precedent as a food source. It is available commonly as a dried powder that contains up to 70 percent protein and it is rich in vitamin B12, beta-carotenes (vitamin A precursors) and minerals, especially iron. It has good digestibility due to an absence of cellulose walls and it contains tocopherols (Vitamin E), gamma linolenic acid and a variety of phenolic acids-vide infra. It has a widespread application as a health food and it is categorized as GRAS by the US Food and Drug Administration (Generally Recognized as Safe). (Karkos P D, et al, Evidence-Based Complementary and Alternative Medicine, Vol, 2011 (2011), Article ID 531053).

Spirulina has been used in several evidence-based applications that are reviewed by Karkos P D et al, ibid, 2011). These applications are reviewed in Table 31.

- Allergy
- Antiviral
- Cholesterol control
- Detoxification
- Bodybuilding
- Rhinitis
  - Diabetes mellitus
- Anticancer effects
  - Antioxidant actions
- Arsenic poisoning

Table 31. Potential applications of spirulina for health (modified from Karkos P D, et al, ibid, 2011).

CHRONIC ARSENIC POISONING AND SPIRULINA

In a randomized clinical trial forty one patients with chronic arsenic poisoning were treated with placebo or spirulina extract (250 mg) combined with zinc (2 mg) twice daily for a period of 16 weeks. The outcome of this treatment regimen was monitored by changes in skin manifestations of arsenic poisoning (melanosis and keratosis) and sequential measurements of arsenic levels in urine and hair samples. Results were favorable in the spiriluna/zinc treated group providing some indication that a spiriluna/zinc mixture may be promising in the normally untreatable condition of arsenic accumulation in humans. (Misbahuddin M, et al, Clinical Toxicology, vol. 44, no. 2, pp 135-141, 2006).

CHRONIC FATIGUE AND SPIRULINA

There are several theoretical reasons why spirulina may increase energy levels, but randomized clinical studies have failed to show this effect in a conclusive manner. (Baicus C, Baicus A, Phytotherapy Research, vol. 21, no. 6, pp 570-573, 2007).

Energy release caused by spirulina may be expected to occur as a result of its easily digested content of essential fats (gamma linolenic acid) and polysaccharides (glycogen and rhamnose). Spirulina may enhance the growth of friendly bacteria in the intestines (Lactobacillus acidopholus) which in turn may increase systemic Vitamin B6 levels that contribute to energy metabolism. However, scores of fatigue in humans are not noted to be increased in small samples (n=4) administered 3 grams per day of spirulina. Much further research is required, because this latter outcome could be a dose-dependent phenomenon.

IMMUNOMODULATION AND SPIRULINA

Spirulina exerts anti-inflammatory effects by reducing histamine release from mast cells. Moreover, randomized double blind controlled clinical trials of spirulina in patients with allergic rhinitis have shown significant changes in immunological parameters in peripheral blood mononuclear cells (Mao T K et al, Journal of Medicinal Food, vol. 8, no. 1, pp 27-30, 2005). These changes involved suppression of IL-4 (interleukin-4) levels which are involved in IgE mediated allergic responses.

The precise mechanisms of the effects of spirulina on immunological parameters requires further delineation, but it is recognized that nutrient support is required to produce optimal functioning of T cell production, secretory IgA responses, cytokine production and Natural Killer cell activity (Karkos PD, et al, ibid, 2001). It is anticipated that spirulina could interact with immune-modulating medications in a positive or negative manner.

SPIRULINA AND BLOOD LIPIDS

The administration of spirulina to individuals with arteriosclerotic, ischemic heart disease has shown favorable reduction in total blood cholesterol, triglycerides and LDL cholesterol with an increase in HDL cholesterol (Ramamoorthy A, Premakumari S, Journal of Food and Science Technology, vol. 33, no. 2, pp 124-128, 1996)(Nakaya N, Atherosclerosis, vol. 37, pp 1329-1337, 1998)(Mani U V, et al Journal of Nutraceuticals, Functional and Medical Foods, vol. 2, no. 3, pp 25-32, 2000).

SPIRULINA AND CANCER

The anti-cancer effects of spirulina remain speculative in the face of limited in vivo evidence for this effect. A major constituent protein (biliprotein) of spirulina called C-phycocyanin (C-PC) has been shown to have antioxidant, anti-inflammatory and direct anti-cancer properties. It is a direct inhibitor of cyclooxygenase type 2 (COX-2) with some apoptosis-inducing properties (Reddy M C, et al, Biochemical and Biophysical Research Communications, Vol. 304, no. 2 p 203).

One notable study of spirulina as a anti-cancer agent has shown regression of oral leukoplakia in 45 percent of subjects after one year's administration of spirulina (Schwartz J and Shklarg, Journal of Oromaxillary Facial Surgery, Vol. 45, no. 6, pp 510-515, 1987 and Schwarz J et al, Nutrition and Cancer, vol. 11, no. 2, pp 127-134, 1988).

SPIRULINA: PROTEIN AND NUTRITIONAL COMPOSITION

As mentioned earlier, dried spirulina contains up to 70 percent protein (range 51-71 percent). It contains all essential amino acids but is somewhat deficient in its content of methionine, cysteine and lysine when compared with egg, meat and dairy protein. That said, spirulina is superior in its amino acid profile compared with many proteins of leguminous origin. Table 32.

AMINO ACID	**AMOUNT (GRAMS)**
Tryptophan	0.93
Threonine	2.97
Isoleucine	3.21
Leucine	4.95
Lysine	3.03
Methionine	1.15
Cystine	0.66
Phenylalanine	2.78
Tyrosine	2.58
Valine	3.51
Arginine	4.15
Histidine	1.01

Alanine	4.52
Aspartic acid	5.79
Glutamic acid	8.39
Glycine	3.10
Proline	2.38
Serine	2.99

Table 32. Protein profiles per 100 gm of spirulina.

In common with several other labeled "plant proteins", spirulina is not a plant protein in the strict sense of definitions. It has a number of other bioactive constituents that distinguish its biological actions Table 33.

PROTEIN: 51-71 percent protein.

LIPID CONTENT: gamma-linolenic acid (GLA), alpha-linolenic acid (ALA), linoleic acid (LA), stearidonic acid (SDA) eicosapentanoic acid (EPA), docosahexanoic acid (DHA) and arachidonic acid (AA).

VITAMIN CONTENT: vitamin B_{12} (an unsuitable source of pseudo-vitamin B_{12}), thiamine (B_1), riboflavin (B_2), nicotinamide (B_3), pyridoxine (B_6), folic acid (B_9), Vitamins A, C, E and K.

MINERALS: potassium, calcium, chromium, copper, iron, magnesium, managanese, phosphorus, selenium, sodium and zinc.

PHYCOBILIPROTEINS: c-phyocyanin, and allophyocyanin.

PIGMENTS: beta-carotene, zeaxthanin, 7-hydroxyretinic acid, chlorophyll-A, xanthophy II, echinenone, myxoxanthophyll, canthaxanthin, diatoxanthin, and 3-hydroxyechinone.

Table 33. Nutritional profile of spirulina.

The World Health Organization (WHO) have endorsed the use of spiriluna as a good nutritional agent, especially in malnourished children (related to its iron and protein content), but concern has been expressed as a result of the contamination of spirulina with certain toxic compounds. In China, there have been reports of contamination of some spirulina with lead, mercury and arsenic.

Some contamination with other toxin producing, blue/green algae may result in the presence of microcystins which are gastrointestinal toxins with some propensity to cause liver cancer with long term exposure. Special care may be required with spirulina usage in patients taking immunosuppressant drugs anticoagulants and in children with the genetic disorder of phenylketonuria.

While considerable promising data about the health benefits of spirulina have emerged in many recent studies, the National institutes of Health have taken a conservative viewpoint on its benefits. This organization denies that there is sufficient scientific evidence to support its use for any specific health disorder, but significant evidence to the contrary does exist (Kulshreshtha A et al, Current Biopharmaceutical Technology 9, (5), 400-405).

CHLORELLA PROTEIN

Chlorella (Chlorella pyrenoidosa) is a good dietary source of protein, fats, carbohydrates, fiber, chlorophyll, vitamins and minerals. A large proportion of the chlorella used in the U.S.A. is grown in Japan or Taiwan (lesser amounts from Korea and China) and it forms a popular dietary supplement that is presented in liquids, tablets or capsules. Chlorella has a reasonable but not complete safety profile. It is most often recommended for short term administration (about 2 months) and its commonest early side effects include diarrhea, gas, nausea and stomach cramping (www.webmd.com/vitamins-supplements/ingredientmono-907-chlorella.aspx?...).

Chlorella has been associated with occasional severe allergic reactions and sun light sensitivity. It is best avoided in individuals with immune disorders as a consequence of unwanted immune regulation (both upregulation or down regulation). This means that immune-regulating drugs may interact with chlorella. Moreover, caution is required with the co-administration of coumadin (warfarin) because of the pro-coagulant vitamin K content of chlorella.

Chlorella is a fresh water, unicellular blue green algae, somewhat similar to spirulina. Several studies have implied that chlorella can provide benefits in promoting cardiovascular health, lowering blood pressure and cholesterol and it may play a special role in managing adverse outcomes of chemotherapy and radiation treatments. It is proposed as an agent to play a role in cancer prevention and to assist in body detoxification of heavy metals. The nutritional composition of chlorella varies considerably depending on circumstances of growth and processing methods. However, on average, it has been estimated that one ounce of high quality chlorella contains: protein (16g), vitamin A (287 percent RDA), vitamin B_2 (71 percent RDA), vitamin B_3 (33 percent RDA), iron (202 percent RDA), magnesium (22 percent RDA), zinc (133 RDA) with supplemental amounts of vitamin B_1, B_6 and phosphorous (draxe.com/7-proven-chlorella-benefits-side-effects). Most commercially produced chlorella is free of major contaminants, but some concerns of heavy metal and pesticide contamination have been expressed about chlorella of Chinese origin, even when it is labelled organic (www.chlorellafactor.com).

It has been reported that marketing claims of pure chlorella (or natural chlorella) have no clear correlation with heavy metal contamination detected in independent laboratory studies. This situation has resulted in suggestions that marketing of much chlorella is performed using "hype" rather than reality. Moreover, a significant amount of chlorella sold in tablet form may be cut with inert filler ingredients, such as calcium carbonate (www.thechlorellafactor.com).

The digestibility of chlorella is important and many sources of information stress the importance of the broken cell wall of chlorella as a determinant of absorption of the nutritional components of chlorella. It has been suggested that certain forms of commercially produced chlorella with thin cell walls is a more important factor in digestibility than the presence of fractured (broken) cell walls.

Based on his recent studies, Mike Adams (editor of naturalnews.com) has concluded several facts about chlorella (Mike Adams, Chlorella Factor, February 19, 2013, www.theclorellafactor.com. According to M. Adams (ibid, 2013).

- *Commercially-grown chlorella is free of mercury.*
- *Chlorella grown in China appears to be the most contaminated with heavy metals.*
- *Chinese chlorella is the cheapest.*
- *Organic chlorella from China is more contaminated than non-organic chlorella from Korea.*
- *Chlorella has been studied in individuals with radiation poisoning, with some benefits.*
- *Cell wall cracking of chlorella to achieve a broken cell wall may improve nutrient absorption but digestibility may be more related to the thickness of the cell wall.*

Much has been written about the compound known as Chlorella Growth Factor (CGF). This substance was first extracted in the 1950's by a Japanese researcher (Fujmaki). It has been demonstrated that this growth factor is expressed during photosynthesis and it drives rapid growth of chlorella. Other researchers have shown that lactobacillus (a friendly gut bacteria) may have its growth stimulated by CGF.

It is proposed that CGF may enhance the functions of nucleic acids in protein synthesis, enzyme production and energy regulation. Moreover, it is claimed that CGF could stimulate tissue repair and have a detoxifying role. Moreover, CGF is a high molecular weight substance that may not be absorbed into the human body in an intact form. In brief, many of the claims made about chlorella as a "superfood" with far-reaching metabolic advantages have not been the subject of detailed clinical research and in some cases they are frankly unsubstantiated.

QUINOA

Quinoa is a food with high nutritive value derived from the species of the plant Chenopodium quinoa W. Quinoa is used often in meals as a cereal, but it does not belong to a grass species of plant and it is often called a pseudocereal. Inter-species hybridization has occurred and considerable advances have been made in the genomics of the plant, its physiology that determines its salt tolerance and its germplasm structures and functions. The plant has been distinguished by having been declared food of the year in 2013 by the Food and Agricultural Organization (FAO) of the United Nations. This occurred for several reasons including: the biodiversity of the plant and its putative role in the quest for food security on a worldwide basis.

Quinoa has an interesting and complex taxonomy. It has been cultivated in the Andes of South America since approximately 3000 years BC by the Incas. The plant is adapted to cold and dry climates and it serves as a primary food source for mountain dwellers who do not have many crops of high nutritional value or diversity. The plant is portable to other climates and locations with growth present in several countries (e.g. the U.S.A., Himalayas, Mexico and Denmark).

There is a great deal of descriptive information about quinoa that is summarized in Table 34.

BENEFITS OF QUINOA	COMMENT
Antioxidant components	The flavonoids quecertin and kaempferol are found in significant concentrations in quinoa and confer general antioxidant properties.
Anti-inflammatory actions	Quinoa contains many anti-inflammatory agents including: polysaccharides, (arabinans and rhamnogolacturonans,

	hydroxycinnamic acid, hydroxybenzoic acids, flavonoids (quecertin and kaempferol), saponins (derived from oleanic acid, hederagenin and serajanic acid, with small amounts of omega 3 fatty acids and alphalinolenic acid.
Inbuilt antioxidant protection	Quinoa has a higher fat content than cereal grasses and it provides monounsaturated fats (MUFA) in the form of oleic acid, together with small amounts of omega 3 fatty acids. The content of antioxidants in quinoa, e.g. tocopherols and, quecertin and kaempferol, prevents rancidity of quinoa and nutrient denaturation during food preparation.

Table 34. Benefits of quinoa.

There are several other health benefits of quinoa which are a common function of its high nutritional value. Quinoa qualifies as a complete protein because the levels of lysine and isoleucine, that are often low in cereals, are substantial in quinoa. The quinoa protein content is complete with a high ratio of protein to carbohydrate as a consequence of the germ making up the 60 percent of the total grain.

Quinoa has a valuable mineral profile. It is high in potassium content. This can assist in blood pressure regulation. Table 35 illustrates the main nutritional components of cooked quinoa, expressed as DRI (daily recommended intake).

COOKED QUINOA   **CALORIES 222**

(0.75 cup, 185 grams)   Low glycemic index

NUTRIENT   **Daily Recommended Intake**

Manganese   59%

Copper	40%
Phosphorus	40%
Magnesium	30%
Fiber	21%
Folate	19%
Zinc	18%

Table 35. Examples of mineral and vitamin content of cooked quinoa expressed as RDI (recommended daily intake) (based on www.whfoods.com/genpage.php? Dbid=142 accessed April 28, 2015).

The high nutritive value of quinoa is illustrated in Table 36 where it is compared with various grains.

	% dry weight					
Crop	Water	Crude Protein	Fat	Carbohy-drates	Fiber	Ash
Quinoa	12.6	13.8	5.0	59.7	4.1	3.4
Barley	9.0	14.7	1.1	67.8	2.0	5.5
Buckwheat	10.7	18.5	4.9	43.5	18.2	4.2
Corn	13.5	8.7	3.9	70.9	1.7	1.2
Millet (Pearl)	11.0	11.9	4.0	68.6	2.0	2.0
Oat	13.5	11.1	4.6	57.6	0.3	2.9
Rice	11.0	7.3	0.4	80.4	0.4	0.5
Rye	13.5	11.5	1.2	69.6	2.6	1.5
Wheat (HRW)	10.9	13.0	1.6	70.0	2.7	1.8

Table 36. Comparisons of nutritional quality (% dry weight of quinoa with various grains. Source of quinoa: Cardoza A. and M. Tapia 1979. Valor nutriva In: Quinoa y Kaniwa. M. Tapia (ed.), Serie Libros y Materiales Educativos No. 49. Reported by J. Risi and H. W. Galwey, 1994. Analyses of the remaining crops reported by: Crampton, E. W. and Harris L. E. 1969. Applied Animal Nutrition, 2nd ed. W. H. Freeman and Co. San Francisco.

Furthermore, the desirable essential amino acid composition of quinoa is shown in comparison with wheat, soy and skim milk in Table 37.

Amino Acid Content (g/100 g protein)				
Amino Acid	Quinoa	Wheat	Soy	Skim Milk
Isoleucine	4.0	3.8	4.7	5.6
Leucine	6.8	6.6	7.0	9.8
Lysine	5.1	2.5	6.3	8.2
Phenylalanine	4.6	4.5	4.6	4.8
Tyrosine	3.8	3.0	3.6	5.0
Cystine	2.4	2.2	1.4	0.9
Methionine	2.2	1.7	1.4	2.6
Threonine	3.7	2.9	3.9	4.6
Tryptophan	1.2	1.3	1.2	1.3
Valine	4.8	4.7	4.9	6.9

Table 37. Essential amino acid pattern of quinoa compared to wheat, soy, skim milk, and the FAO reference patterns (1973) for evaluating proteins. Source: Johnson R. and R. Anguilera 1980. Processing Varieties of Oilseeds (Lupin and Quinoa). In: Report to Natural Fibers and Foods Commission of Texas, 1978-1980 (Reported by D. Cusack, 1984, The Ecologist 14:21-31).

Quinoa contains a group of glycoside compounds called saponins. These are foaming compounds that were once used to produce soap. Saponins are removed from quinoa by soaking prior to cooking. Primary saponin compounds in quinoa include oleanic acid, hederagenin and phytolaccagenic acid. These compounds have a variety of uses or properties. Their medicinal uses include: antifungal agents, antiviral medicines, anti-bacterial compounds, insecticides, anti-helminthics and immune stimulators. In addition, oleanic acid may act as a hepatic protectant, an anti-inflammatory agent and an antioxidant with some cancer protective effects.

Saponins have been described as possessing a degree of toxicity. Although saponins are toxic when given by injection, they are not well absorbed via the oral route. Moreover, other plant saponins appear to increase mineral absorption (e.g. calcium and silicon). Overall, the risks from eating saponins in quinoa are not considered to have significant consequences if the quinoa is prewashed and there is no excessive consumption of the leaves of the plant (www.glutenfreegigi.com/quesitonable-quinoa-perfect-plant-protein-or-poison, accessed May 4, 2015).

MYCOPROTEIN (QUORN)

Mycoprotein cannot be considered to be a plant protein given its origin from the fungus called Fusarium venenatum. It is a meat-free source of protein that supplies a beneficial amount of dietary fiber. Fusarium venenatum is a common type of fungus which is part of the family of other fungi, including morels and truffles. The structure of the fungus consists of a web of hyphae which are present as an aggregate of thin, spun strands. The resemblance of mycoprotein to meat is due to the filamentous structure of the hyphae of the fungus which bears resemblance to bundles of muscle fibers (www.mycoprotein.org).

Mycoprotein has several health benefits including the promotion of a healthy blood cholesterol, significant induction of satiety following ingestion and a low glycemic index. The key health benefits of mycoprotein are listed in table 38.

- Mycoprotein contains all essential amino acids.
- Mycoprotein is high in dietary fiber and slows gastric emptying while avoiding constipation.
- Mycoprotein is low in sodium and fats. It does not contain cholesterol or trans-fats.
- Mycoprotein has a tendency to induce feelings of fullness after eating (satiety induction).
- Mycoprotein may help regulate blood glucose levels by virtue of its low glycemic index.
- Mycoprotein is a complete protein containing all essential amino acids.

Table 38. Health benefits of mycoprotein (adapted from www.mycoprotein .org).

CHOLESTEROL AND SATIETY CONTROL WITH MYCOPROTEIN

Several studies (Turnbull et al, Am J. Clin. Nutr., 55, 415-9, 1992) show that mycoprotein may lower total blood cholesterol and LDL (low density lipoprotein). When eaten with a balanced low fat diet, mycoprotein may play a special role in managing diabetes mellitus. It appears that fiber contained with mycoprotein exerts a greater effect on satiety than several other types of fiber (Burley et al Eur. J. Clin. Nutr. 47, 409-418, 1993 and Turnbull et al Am. J. Clin Nutr, 58, 507-10, 1993).

MYCOPROTEIN AND BLOOD SUGAR

A reduction in post-prandial glucose and insulin levels can be expected to occur following a significant amount of ingestion of mycoprotein. Together with effects of mycoprotein on blood glucose and satiety it is proposed that this food may be useful in the management of obesity. The assistance of mycoprotein with blood glucose regulation is valuable in the management of diabetes mellitus, in the absence of delayed gastric emptying due to diabetic gastroparesis. A further potential benefit of mycoprotein is to assist in overcoming insulin resistance which is a principal component of Metabolic Syndrome X. There have been some allergies described with mycoprotein that may limit its use, but the prevalence of such allergies has not been studied in detail.

POTATO PROTEIN

Potatoes present a high dietary load of rapidly digested starch. For example, one large baked russet potato presents approximately 290 calories of which about 64 grams are carbohydrates. The rapid rate and amount of digestion of potato starch cause a high glycemic index rating for the potato which may tend to produce elevated blood sugar and promote insulin resistance (Sandi Busch: helathyeating.sfgate.com/muchprotein...), (www.livestrong.com/article/366913-the-protein-content-of-potatoes).

The protein content of potatoes is relatively small and potato protein is not a complete protein. For example, a three ounce portion contains about 1.75 to 2.25 gram of protein. A three ounce portion of potato provides less than 5 percent of daily protein needs in many circumstances (www.livestrong.com/article/366913-the-protein-content-of-potatoes/).

Although only about 2 percent of a potato is protein, it presents a good dietary carbohydrate to protein ratio. Potato protein is of high quality, but it is classified as incomplete because of small contents of certain amino acids. Comparisons of potato protein with rice and cereal protein shows that it has a higher lysine content but a lower cysteine content. Thus, their appear to be some advantages of combining certain carbohydrates to enhance protein content of meals (www.thedailyspud.com/2011/01/6/potatoes-nutritionfacts/).

Food ranking systems show potatoes to be a source of vitamin B_6, potassium, copper, vitamin C, manganese, phosphorus, niacin, dietary-fiber and pantothenic acid. Moreover, potatoes contain several phytonutrients, some of which are antioxidants. Examples of phytonutrients in potatoes include carotenoids, flavonoids and coffeic acid. One notable antioxidant compound in potatoes is patatin (a unique storage protein)(Liu Y W, Han C H, Lee M H et al, Patatin, the Fiber Storage Protein of Potato, Exhibits Antioxidant Activity, J.Agric. Food Chem 2003, 51 (15): 4389-93).

Apart from the general nutrient value of potatoes, research has shown the presence of kukoamines in potatoes (Parr A, Mellon F, Colquhoun I, Davies H Dihydrocaffeoyl Polyamines (Kukoamine and Allies) in Potato (Solanum tuberosum) Tubers Detected during Metabolic Profiling. J. Agric. Food Chem, 53, (13), 5461-5466, 2005). Scientists at the UK, Institute for Food Research (IFR) have identified blood pressure lowering ability of kukoamines and their pharmacodynamics characteristics.

NUTS

There are a wide variety of nuts in the food chain, but generalizations about their health value can be made from many studies. A number of population studies (epidemiological studies) shown that the higher the nut intake the lower the occurrence of ischemic heart disease and obesity. In addition, regular nut intake has beneficial effects in several areas of health promotion Table 39.

- Improved nutritional status
- Lower obesity rates

- Lower blood pressure
- Low incidence of cardiovascular disease

- Reduction in blood lipids
- Antioxidant effects

- Increase longevity
- Reduction of inflammation

- Improved endothelial (function)

Table 39. The beneficial health effects of nut intake (adapted from the Nut Research Group, University of Otago, www.otago.ac.nz/human nutrition/research/nut.

Cumulative research at the University of Otago in New Zealand have shown several findings that are summarized in table 40.

- All forms of raw nuts improves cardiovascular risk factors and this effect is most notable in patients with cardiovascular risk factors such as abnormal blood cholesterol profiles.
- A barrier to nut consumption is the perception that they may cause weight gain, but intakes of nuts up to 60 grams per day does not adversely effect body weight.
- Eating nuts is acceptable to many people and it is a readily sustainable dietary habit.
- Nuts are a concentrated source of health-giving nutrients, e.g. unsaturated fat, fiber, vitamin E and minerals, e.g. selenium in Brazil nuts.

Table 40. Principal research findings of the University of Otago, concerning nut consumption (www.otago.ac.nz/ibid).

An excellent source of information on the health benefits of nuts is found in the book Preedy V et al (editors) Nuts and Seeds in Health Disease Prevention, San Diego, Academic Press (2010). It is not possible to discuss individual studies on specific nuts in several disease states in this short book. Table 41 gives a list of different nuts and illustrates that each type of nut may have specific health benefits as a consequence of their different nutritional profiles. Nut research is often grouped with research on seed intake due to considerable similarities in beneficial nutritional profiles (table 41).

NUT/SEED	COMMENT
Almonds	Studies show a reduction in markers of oxidative stress with a one month intake of almonds daily (Jenkins D J et al, J. Nutr. 138, 908-13, 2008)
Walnuts	Protect against breast cancer and assist in blood pressure regulation by enhancing blood vessel dilation in diabetics (May Y et al Diabetes Care, 33, 227-232, 2010).
Pistachios and Mediterranean Pine Nuts	Assist in lowering blood cholesterol by virtue of their sterol contents (Ellegard, L H et al Nutr. Rev., 65, 39-45, 2007). Pistachios reduce oxidative stress, inflammation and cholesterol (Kay C et al, J. Nutr. 140, 1093-1098, 2010).
Mediterranean Pine Nuts	Tend to curb appetite and increase satiety (Pasman W J et al, Lipids in Health and Disease, 7, 10-14, 2008).
Seeds of flax, chia and hemp	Substantial contents of omega 3 fatty acids and hemp seed protein and has a special role in athletic pursuits.
Pumpkin seeds	Are rich in iron and may prevent prostate cancer (Hong H et al, Nutr. Res. Pract., 3, 323-7, 2009).
Sesame seeds	A rich source of calcium with lignans and vitamin E (Higdon J, Evidence Based Approach to Dietary Phytochemicals, NY, Thieme, 2006).

Table 41. Nuts and seeds that have specific beneficial health effects (adapted from www.drfuhrman.com/library/nuts-seeds.aspx).

NUT ALLERGIES

Allergic responses to peanuts and tree nuts are among the most common food allergies which can occasionally be very severe, resulting in anaphylaxis. An individual with one type of nut allergy is more likely to be allergic to other types of nuts. In some cases, even trace amounts of nuts can trigger allergy and this is especially true of peanuts (an example of a legume). Recent studies imply that 25-40 percent of individuals who have peanut allergy are also allergic to tree nuts (almonds, walnuts, cashews, etc.). (Scherer S H et al J. Allergy Clin Immunol., 125 (6), 1322-6, 2010).

A person with allergies to tree nuts or peanuts are often advised to avoid other nuts that are listed in Table 42.

Almond	Nangai nut
Artificial nuts	Nut extracts
Brazil nuts	Nut butters
Beechnut	Nut meal
Butternut	Nut meat
Cashew	Nut milk
Chestnut	Nut paste
Chinquapin	Nut pieces
Coconut	Pecan
Hazelnut	Pesto
Gianduja	Pilinut
Gingko nut	Pine nut
Hickory	Pistachio

Lichee	Praline
Macadamia	Sheanut
Marzipan	Walnut

Table 42. The wide range of potential dietary sources of nuts is apparent and cross allergenicity may exist among tree nuts (adapted from www.foodallergy.org/allergens/tree-nut-allergy.

BUCKWHEAT

Misunderstood as a cereal grain, buckwheat is actually a fruit seed related to rhubarb and sorrel. It is valuable as an alternative for individuals with gluten enteropathy. Studies have shown that buckwheat may lower total blood cholesterol, lower LDL cholesterol and increase the ratio of HDL to LDL, thereby lowering key cardiovascular risk factors.

The nutritional benefits of buckwheat are bolstered by its high content of rutin which complements the antioxidant functions of vitamin C, (in common with other flavonoids found in buckwheat). Flavonoids are effective at reducing platelet aggregation and promoting healthy blood flow. The high content of magnesium has other cardiovascular benefits including lowering blood pressure and generally improving blood flow.

Buckwheat may promote satiety and it has a low glycemic index. Moreover, large population studies have shown that buckwheat may prevent type 2 diabetes mellitus as a presumed consequence of its effects on blood glucose control and its magnesium content. Moreover, recent studies have shown that buckwheat contains an anti-diabetic agent called chiro-inositol which appears to act on blood glucose regulation. Other benefits of buckwheat include: the prevention of gallstones, cancer prevention (colon cancer and breast cancer) and significant cardiovascular protection with breast cancer prevention in post-menopausal females.

Table 43 shows the individual amounts of amino acids in one cup (168g) of buckwheat. Buckwheat is not a complete protein because of limiting amino acid contents.

AMINO ACID	AMOUNT	AMINO ACID	AMOUNT
Alanine	0.32g	Lysine	0.29g
Arginine	0.42g	Methionine	0.07g
Aspartic acid	0.49g	Phenylalanine	0.22g
Cysteine	0.10g	Proline	0.22g
Glutamic acid	0.88g	Serine	0.29g
Glycine	0.44g	Threonine	0.22g
Histidine	0.13g	Tryptophan	0.08g
Isoleucine	0.21g	Tyrosine	0.10g
Leucine	0.36g	Valine	0.29G

Table 43. Individual amino acid content of buckwheat (1 cup, 168 grams) (adapted from www.whfoods.com/gen-page.php?tname, accessed May 2, 2015.

LENTILS

Lentils are examples of edible pulses (Lens culinaris) (www.whfoods.com, accessed 5/3/15. They grow as bushy annual plants and vary in color (yellow, red, green orange and black). They are supplied whole or split and vary considerably in size. Lentils are a good source of essential nutrients including protein, dietary fiber, folate, thiamin, phosphorus and iron (www.whfoods.com, ibid 2015).

The presence of slowly digested and resistant starch give lentils special properties as a functional food, with uses in diabetes mellitus and as a prebiotic. There are a number of antinutrient components in lentil starch including phytates and trypsin inhibitors. Phytates can be removed to a variable degree by pre-soaking for about 12 hours. The largest producer of lentils is Canada followed closely by India. Nutritional facts for lentils are shown in table 44.

SERVING SIZE	198 GRAMS
Calories	230
Total fat	1 % (one gram)
Cholesterol	0%
Sodium	4 mg
Total Carbohydrate	40 grams 13% RDI
Dietary fiber	16 grams 63% RDI
Sugars	4 grams
Protein	18 grams
Vitamin C	5% RDI
Calcium	4% RDI
Iron	37% RDI

Table 44. Nutrition facts panel for lentils.

Lentils do not contain a complete protein due to a lack of the amino acids methionine and cysteine, but sprouted lentils do contain all nine essential amino acids. Rice protein is a good complementary protein to use with lentils. Studies show that lentils are an excellent source of trace minerals e.g. molybdenum (330% RDI), copper (56% RDI), manganese (49% RDI), iron (37% RDI), and zinc (25% RDI).

One concern about lentils is their high content of purines. Purines are broken down in the body to produce uric acid and hyperuricemia is associated with renal stones and the development of gout. It is suggested that purines from plant food are less likely to cause manifestations of elevated blood uric acid than animal proteins from meat, poultry and fish. The breakdown of amino acids found in lentils is shown in table 45.

AMINO ACID	AMOUNT	AMINO ACID	AMOUNT
Alanine	0.75	Phenylalanine	0.88
Arginine	1.38	Proline	0.75

Aspartic acid	1.98	Serine	0.82
Cysteine	0.23	Threonine	0.64
Glutamic acid	2.77	Tryptophan	0.16
Glycine	0.73	Tyrosine	0.48
Histidine	0.50	Valine	0.89
Leucine	1.29	Lysine	1.25
		Methionine	0.15

Table 45. Individual amino acid contents of lentils data are "average" in amount (adapted from www.whfoods.com/gen page.php?t name=foodspice and dbid=52).

BEANS

Beans come in many varieties, including soybeans. Beans are rich in protein and are often underestimated as a dietary source of protein. Moreover, beans are low in fat, high in fiber and micronutrients. Soybeans contain complete proteins but other beans do not (www.healthyeating.sfgate.com). However, beans are high in lysine which is often limited in its amount in other plant proteins. Beans and rice are ideal complementary sources of protein. The protein contents of beans (except soybeans) are reported somewhat inaccurately as one generic value Table 46.

BEAN	AMOUNT OF PROTEIN PER CUP
White, adzuki, pinto, kidney, black navy garbanzo and lima	15 grams/average
White beans	17.4 grams
Lima beans	10.3 grams
Others	15-17 grams

Table 46. Total content of protein in different kinds of beans. On average the protein content is abut 15 grams (adapted from www.healthyeating.sfgate.com/types-beans-highest-amount-protein-6835.html, accessed 5/3/15).

The nutritional contents and amino acid profiles of many beans and legumes can be accessed through the website http/nutritionaldata.self.com/facts/legumes.

CHICKPEAS (GARBANZO BEANS)

Chickpeas are legumes that belong to the genus Fabaceae. They are sometimes called garbanzo beans, kabuli, gram or Egyptian peas. Garbanzo beans are best recognized for the nutritional quality of high fiber content. They contain about 12.5 grams of fiber per cup (50% of the RDI of fiber). A large portion of the fiber content is insoluble and moves into the colon where it promotes the growth of friendly bacteria (a prebiotic effect). The metabolic end products of this process are short chain fatty acids (acetic acid, butyric acid and propionic acid). Butyric acid is a principal energy substitute for colonic epithelial cells that benefit from the administration of chickpeas.

In addition to the promotion of colonic health, chickpeas supply several antioxidants, assist in lowering blood cholesterol and help to control spikes in blood glucose. One major benefit of garbanzo beans is the promotion of satiety which may decrease overall calorie intake and help to prevent obesity. Such benefits are common to legumes and other plant proteins (www.whfoods.com/genpage, php? tname).

Garbanzo beans are a good source of antioxidants with a content of several bioactive free-radical scavaging phytonutrients. These phytonutrients include quercetin, kaempferol and myricetin. The interior of the bean is rich in phenolic acids such as ferulic acid, chlorogenic acid, caffeic acid and vanillic acid (www.whfoods.com). The substantial load of antioxidants in chickpeas results in cardioprotection and reduction in levels of oxidized LDL. These effects are complemented by the presence of manganese that supports mitochondrial (energy production) and acts as valuable antioxidant (www.whfoods.com).

FAVA BEANS

Fava beans (Vicia faba or broad beans) are a source of fiber, protein and folic acid. The nutritional content of a one cup serving of fresh fava beans (boiled) includes: 33 grams of carbohydrate, 13 grams of protein, 1 gram of fat; and it delivers 187 calories. This serving size of fava bean contains 177 micrograms of folate which is equivalent to 44 percent of the RDA of folate (based on a 2000 calorie diet). Fava beans are mineral rich with variable contents of calcium, potassium, manganese, but fresh beans are low in sodium (8 mg of sodium). However, canned fava beans are high in sodium content. It is proposed that fava beans are nutrient dense with potential benefits for cardiovascular health.

Table 47 gives a comparison of the protein content of several types of beans. Table 47 shows that soy beans are the highest in protein content and the protein is of premium quality, containing all nine essential amino acids.

TYPE OF BEAN	AMOUNT (COOKED) (Grams) (Approx. one cup)	PROTEIN CONTENT (Grams)
Soybean	172	29
Edamame	180	22
Lentils	198	17
Red Kidney Bean	177	16
Fava Beans	170	13
Black Beans	172	15
Navy Beans	172	15
Haricot Beans	182	15
Black-eyed Peas	170	14
Garbanzos	164	14
Lima Beans	170	14

Table 47. The approximate protein content (grams) per one cup serving approximately of various beans.

Beans do not contain complete proteins. Fava beans are low in the essential amino acids methionine and tryptophan. Moreover, Fava beans contain specific bioactive compounds including isoflavones and associated plant sterols. The isoflavone content is similar to soybeans with the presence of genistein and daidzein. The beans also contain the valuable phytosterol, named beta-sitosterol which can assist in cholesterol reduction and the promotion of healthy prostate structure and function. Fava beans contain L-Dopa which is a neurochemical precursor of dopamine, epinephrine and nor-epinephrine. The role of fava bean consumption in the prevention of disorders associated with depleted dopamine (Parkinson's disease and certain types of dystonia) remains underexplored.

Fava beans are quite toxic in individuals with genetic defects that result in glucose-6 phosphate dehydrogenase enzyme deficiency (G6PD deficiency). This genetic disorder results in a potential compromise of the oxygen carrying capacity of the blood with the development of hemolytic anemia. Raw fava beans contain alkaloids (vicine and convicine) which initiate hemolytic anemic in G6PD deficient individuals. Fava beans together with certain drugs (e.g. dapsone) and infections can precipitate problems of "favism" in individuals with G6PD deficiency.

Fava beans are a potential source of excess oxalic acid in the diet, as a consequence of their high purine content. The consumption of several beans of the Fabaceae family and vegetables of the Brassica group may contribute to hyperoxaluria and the formation of oxalate stones in the urinary tract. In addition, fava beans are a source of tyramine which causes serious adverse effects in individuals taking monoamine oxidase inhibiting drugs.

NUTRITIONAL YEAST

Nutritional yeast is clearly not a plant protein. The two main types of nutritional yeast are Brewer's yeast and pure nutritional yeast. Consumers have confused these food products with Candida albicans (thrush) which causes a variety of symptoms, signs and diseases as common opportunistic pathogen. In contrast, nutritional yeast is health giving and acts as a powerhouse of essential vitamins and minerals table 48.

- A wide spectrum of B vitamins.
- Chromium for glucose regulation and potential for weight control.
- At least sixteen individual amino acids.
- At least fourteen key minerals.
- A rich source of phosphorus
- Beneficial effects on glucose tolerance (Offenbacher EG, Pi-Sunyer FX, Diabetes 29, 11, 919-25, 1980).

Table 48. Nutritional aspects of nutritional yeast (adapted from wwwkimberlysnyder.com/blog/2014/09/08/inconvenient-truth-nutritional-yeast/).

CRANBERRY PROTEIN

Cranberry protein powder is a recent development in the food industry. It has several advantages including: a potential alternative to avoid allergens in popular protein powders, such as soy and whey. It is produced by cold extrusion and filtration, thereby avoid enzymatic or solvent extraction methods. This innovative source of protein contains up to 30 percent protein with up to 20 percent soluble fiber and up to 47 percent insoluble fiber. The powder has about 1 percent omega 3 and omega 6 fatty acids with about 0.75 percent omega 9 fatty acids.

Cranberry extracts are high in bioflavonoids and they have an attractive amino acid profile (Table 49).

AMINO ACID	AMOUNT (g/100g)
Tyrosine	0.5 - 2
Gutamic acid	5 - 7
Phenylatanine	1 - 3
Glycine	1 - 3
Alanine	1 - 3
Cysteine	0.3-2

Table 49. Amino acid profile of cranberry protein powder (nutraingredients-usa.com).

Important components of cranberry protein powder include proanthocyanidins (PAC) which have a protective benefit against urinary tract infections. These PAC have anti-adhesion properties with actions against common human bacteria that can cause urinary tract infections.

CONCLUSION

Further research will assist in the definition of the actions of several plant and related proteins with health giving effects. Different plants contain several health giving phytonutrients.

REFERENCES: OTHER PROTEINS

Aider, M.; Barbana, C.; Canola Proteins: Composition, extraction, functional properties, bioactivity, application as a food ingredient and allergenicity- a practical and critical review, Trends Food Sci Tech, 2011, 22, pp. 21-39).

Alvarez-Jubete L. Wijngaard H, Arendt EK et al. Polyphenol composition and in vitro antioxidant activity of amaranth, quinoa buckwheat and wheat as affected by sprouting and baking. Food Chemistry, Volume 119, Issue 2, 15 March 2010, Pages 770-778, 2010.

Baer HJ, Glynn RJ, Hu FB, et al: Risk factors for mortality in the nurses' health study: a competing risks analysis. *Am J Epidemiol* 2011;173:319-329.

Baehr M, Fechner A, Jahreis G: The potential of lupin protein to exert antiatherosclerotic effects (abstract). Atheroscler Suppl 2013. In press.

Bahr, M.; Fechner, A.; Kramer, J.; Kientopf, M.; Jahreis, G.; Nutrition Journal, 2013, 12, 107.

Baicus C, Baicus A, Phytotherapy Research, vol. 21, no. 6 pp 570-573, 2007.

Belski R, Mori TA, Puddeu IB, Sipsas S, Woodman RJ, Ackland TR, Beilin LJ, Dove ER, Carlyon NB, Jayaseena V, Hodgson JM: Effects of lupin-enriched foods on body composition and cardiovascular disease risk factors: a 12-month randomized controlled weight loss trial. Int J Obes 2011, 35:810-819.

Bos C, Airinei G, Mariotti F, Benamouzig R, Berot S, Evrard J, et al. The poor digestibility of rapeseed protein is balanced by its very high metabolic utilization in humans. J Nutr. 2007:137:594-600.

Buck K, Vrieling A, Zaineddin AK, et al: Serum enterolactone and prognosis of postmenopausal breast cancer. *J Clin Oncol* 2011;29:3730-3738.

Burley et al Eur. J. Clin. Nutr. 47, 409-418, 1993.

Cam A, De Mejia EG: Role of dietary proteins and peptides in cardiovascular disease. Mol Nutr Food Res 2012, 56:53-66.

Cumby N, Zhong Y, Naczk M, Shahidi F. Antioxidant activity and water-holding capacity of canola protein hydrolysates. Food Chem. 2008;109:144-148.

Chisholm A, Mann J, Skeaff M, Frampton C, Sutherland W, Duncan A, Tiszavari S. A diet rich in walnuts favourably influences plasma fatty acid profile in moderately hyperlipidaemic subjects. Eur J Clin Nutr 1998;52:12-6.

Dini I, Tenore GC, and Dini A. Antioxidant compound contents and antioxidant activity before and after cooking in sweet and bitter Chenopodium quinoa seeds. LWT – Food Science and Technology, Volume 43, Issue 3, April 2010, Pages 447-451, 2010.

Dini I, Tenore GC, and Dini A. Antioxidant compound contents and antioxidant activity before and after cooking in sweet and bitter Chenopodium quinoa seeds. LWT - Food Science and Technology, Volume 43, Issue 3, April 2010, Pages 447-451. 2010.

Duranti M, Morazzoni P: Nutraceutical properties of lupin seed proteins: a great potential still waiting for full exploitation. Agro Food Industry Hi-Tech 2011, 22:20-23.

Ellegard LH, Andersson SW, Normen AL, et al: Dietary plant sterols and cholesterol metabolism. *Nutr Rev* 2007;65:39-45.

Fleddermann, M. et al, Nutritional evaluation of rapeseed protein compared to soy protein for quality, plasma amino acids, and nitrogen balance- A randomized cross-over intervention study in humans, Clinical Nutrition, Vol. 32, Issue 4, pp. 519-526, August 2013.

Fraser GE, Shavlik DJ: Ten years of life: Is it a matter of choice? *Arch Intern Med* 2001;161:1645-1652.

Gee JM, Price KR, Ridout CL et al. Saponins of quinoa (Chenopodium quinoa): effects of processing on their abundance in quinoa products and their biological effects on intestinal mucosal tissue. Journal of the Science of Food and Agriculture 63. 2 (1993): 201-209. 1993.

Guasch-Ferre M, Bullo M, Martinez-Gonzalez MA, et al: Frequency of nut consumption and mortality risk in the PREDIMED nutrition intervention trial. *BMC Med* 2013;11:164.

Higdon J: Lignans. In *An Evidence-Based Approach to Dietary Phytochemicals.* New York: Thieme; 2006: 155-161

Hirose Y, Fujita T, Ishii T et al. Antioxidative properties and flavonoid composition of Chenopodium quinoa seeds cultivated in Japan. . Food Chemistry, Volume 119, Issue 4, 15 April 2010, Pages 1300-1306. 2010.

Hodgson JM, Lee YP, Puddey IB, Sipsas S, Ackland TR, Beilin LJ, Belski R, Mori TA: Effects of increasing dietary protein and fiber intake with lupin on body weight and composition and blood lipids in overweight men and women. Int J Obes 2010, 34:1086-1094.

Hong H, Kim CS, Maeng S: Effects of pumpkin seed oil and saw palmetto oil in Korean men with symptomatic benign prostatic hyperplasia. *Nutr Res Pract* 2009;**3:**323-327.

Hu FB: Protein, body weight, and cardiovascular health. Am J Clin Nutr 2005, 82:242S-247S.

James LEA. Chapter 1: Quinoa (Chenopodium quinoa Willd.): Composition, Chemistry, Nutritional, and Functional Properties. Advances in Food and Nutrition Research, Volume 58, 2009, Pages 1-31. 2009.

Jancurova M, Minarovicova L and Dandar A. Quinoa - a review. Czech J. Food Sci. 2009, 27: 71-79. 2009.

Jenkins DJ, Kendall CW, Marchie A, et al: Almonds reduce biomarkers of lipid peroxidation in older hyperlipidemic subjects. *J Nutr* 2008;138:908-913.

Kay CD, Gebauer SK, West SG, et al: Pistachios increase serum antioxidants and lower serum oxidized-LDL in hypercholesterolemic adults. *J Nutr* 2010;140:1093-1098.

Khattab RY, Arnfield SD. Functional properties of raw and processed canola meal. LWT-Food Sci Technol. 2009;42:1119-1124.

Kohajdova Z, Karovicova J, Schmidt S: Lupin composition and possible use in bakery-a review.

Kocyigit A, Koylu AA, Keles H: Effects of pistachio nuts consumption on plasma lipid profile and oxidative status in healthy volunteers. *Nutrition, metabolism, and cardiovascular diseases : NMCD* 2006;16:202-209.

Kracht W, Danicke S, Kluge H, Keller K, Matzke W, Hennig U. Effect of dehulling of rapeseed on feed value and nutrient digestibility of rape products in pigs. Arch Anim Nutr. 2004;58:389-404.

Kris-Etherton PM, Hu FB, Ros E, et al: The role of tree nuts and peanuts in the prevention of coronary heart disease: multiple potential mechanisms. *J Nutr* 2008;138:1746S-1751S.

Kulshreshtha A et al, Current Biopharmaceutical Technology 9, (5), 400-405.

Ma Y, Njike VY, Millet J, et al: Effects of walnut consumption on endothelial function in type 2 diabetic subjects: a randomized controlled crossover trial. *Diabetes Care* 2010;33:227-232.

Lee YP, Mori TA, Puddey IB, Sipsas S, Ackland TR, Beilin LJ, Hodgson JM: Effects of lupin kernel flour-enriched bread on blood pressure: a controlled intervention study. Am J Clin Nutr 2009, 89:766-772.

Leupp, JL, Lardy GP, Soto-Navarro SA, Bauer ML, Caton JS. Effects of canola seed supplementation on intake, digestion, duodenal protein supply, and microbial efficiency in steers fed forage-based diets. J Anim Sci. 2006:84:499-507.

Liu Y W, Han C H, Lee M H et al, Patatin, the Fiber Storage Protein of Potato, Exhibits Antioxidant Activity, J.Agric. Food Chem 2003, 51 (15): 4389-93).

Mani U V, et al Journal of Nutraceuticals, Functional and Medical Foods, vol. 2, no. 3, pp 25-32, 2000. Mansour EH, Dworsvhak E, Lugasi A, Gaal O, Barna E, Gergely A. Effect of processing on the antinutritive factors and nutritive value of rapeseed products. Food Chem. 1993;47:247-252.

Mao T K et al, Journal of Medicinal Food, vol. 8, no. 1, pp 27-30, 2005.

Mariotti F, Pueyo ME, Tome D, Mahe S. The bioavailability and postprandial utilization of sweet lupin-flour protein is similar to that of purified soyabean protein in human subjects: as study using intrinsically 15N-labelled proteins. Brit j Nutr. 2002;87:315-323.

Misbahuddin M, et al, Clinical Toxicology, vol. 44, no. 2, pp 135-141, 2006.

Nakaya N, Atherosclerosis, vol. 37, pp 1329-1337, 1998.

Naruszewicz M, Nowicka G, Klosiewicz-Latoszek L, Arnoldi A, Sirtori C: Effect of lupin protein (Lupinus albus) on cardiovascular risk factors in smokers with mild hypercholesterolemia (abstract). Circulation 2006, 114:874-874.

Parr A, Mellon F, Colquhoun I, Davies H, Dihydrocaffeoyl Polyamines (Kukoamine and Allies) in Potato (Solanum tuberosum) Tubers Detected during Metabolic Profiling. J. Agric. Food Chem, 53, (13), 5461-5466, 2005).

Pasman WJ, Heimerikx J, Rubingh CM, et al: The effect of Korean pine nut oil on in vitro CCK release, on appetite sensations and on gut hormones in post-menopausal overweight women. *Lipids in Health and Disease* 2008;**7**:10.

Preedy V et al (editors) Nuts and Seeds in Health Disease Prevention, San Diego, Academic Press (2010).

Processing Varieties of Oilseeds (Lupin and Quinoa). In: Report to Natural Fibers and Foods Commission of Texas, 1978-1980 (Reported by D. Cusack, 1984, The Ecologist 14:21-31).

Rajaram S, Sabate J: Nuts, body weight and insulin resistance. *Br J Nutr* 2006;96 Suppl 2:S79-86.

Ramamoorthy A, Premakumari S, Journal of Food and Science Technology, vol. 33, no. 2, pp 124-128, 1996.

Repo-Carrasco-Valencia R, Hellstrom JK, Pihlava JM et al. Flavonoids and other phenolic compounds in Andean indigenous grains: Quinoa (Chenopodium quinoa), kaniwa (Chenopodium pallidicaule) and kiwicha (Amaranthus caudatus). Food Chemistry, Volume 120, Issue 1, 1 May 2010, Pages 128-133. 2010.

Repo-Carrasco-Valencia RA, EncinaRepo-Carrasco-Valencia RA, Encina CR, Binaghi MJ et al. CR, Effects . Effects of roasting and boiling of quinoa, kiwicha and kaniwa on composition and availability of minerals in vitro. J Sci Food Agric. 2010 Sep;90(12):2068-73. 2010.

Ros E: Nuts and novel biomarkers of cardiovascular disease. *Am J Clin Nutr* 2009;89:1649S-1656S.

Salas-Salvado J, Casas-Agustench P, Murphy MM, et al: The effect of nuts on inflammation. *Asia Pac J Clin Nutr* 2008;17 Suppl 1:333-336.

Sandi Busch: healthyeating.sfgate.com/muchprotein....)(www.livestrong.com/article/366913-the-protein-content-of-potatoes).

Sari I, Baltaci Y, Bagci C, et al: Effect of pistachio diet on lipid parameters, endothelial function, inflammation, and oxidative status: a prospective study. *Nutrition* 2010;26:399-404.

Scherer S H et al J. Allergy Clin Immunol., 125 (6), 1322-6, 2010.

Schwartz J and Shklarg, Journal of Oromaxillary Facial Surgery, Vol. 45, no. 6, pp 510-515, 1987.

Schwarz J et al, Nutrition and Cancer, vol. 11, no. 2, pp 127-134, 1988.

Sharma KD, Bindal G, Rathour R et al. Beta-Carotene and mineral content of different Chenopodium species and the effect of cooking on micronutrient retention. . Int J Food Sci Nutr. 2012 May;63(3):290-5. Epub 2011 Oct 10. 2012.

Sirtori, C.R.; Lovati, M.R.; Manzoni, C.; Castiglioni, S.; Duranti, M.; Magni, C.; Morandi, S.; D'Agostina, A.; and Arnoldi, A.; J. Nutr., Jan., 2004, vol 134, 8-23.

Sirtori CR, Triolo M, Bosiso R, Bondioli A, Calabresi L, De Vergori V, Gomaraschi M, Mombelli G, Pazzucconi F, Zacherl C, Arnoldi A: Hypocholesterolaemic effects of lupin protein and pea prodein/fibre combinations in moderately hypercholesterolaemic individuals. Br J Nutr 2012, 107:1176-1183.

Sirtori CR, Gallli C, Anderson JW, Arnoldi: Nutritional and nutraceutical approaches to dyslipidemia and atherosclerosis prevention: Focus on dietary proteins.

Sirtori CR, Lovati MR, Manzoni C, Castiglioni S, Duranti M, Magni C, Morandi S, D'Agostina A, Arnoldi A: Proteins of white lupin seed, a naturally isoflavone-poor legume, reduce cholesterolemia in rats and increase LDL receptor activity in HepG2 cells.

Teunissen-Beekman KF, Van Baak MA: The role of dietary protein in blood pressure regulation. Curr Opin Lipidol 2013, 24:65-70

Tey SL, Brown R, Chisholm A, Gray A, Williams S, Delahunty C. Current guidelines for nut consumption are achievable and sustainable: a hazelnut intervention. Br J Nutr 2011b;105:1503-11.

Tey SL, Brown R, Gray A, Chisholm A, Delahunty C. Nuts improve diet quality compared to other energy-dense snacks while maintaining body weight. J Nutr Metab 2011c;2011:357350.

Tey SL, Brown RC, Gray AR, Chisholm AW, Delahunty CM. Long-term consumption of high energy-dense snack foods on sensory-specific satiety and intake. Am J Clin Nutr 2012;95:1038-47.

Thomson CD. Brazil nuts (Bertholletia excelsa): improved selenium status and other health benefits. In: Preedy VR, Watson RR, Patel VB, editors. Nuts and seeds in health and disease prevention. San Diego: Academic Press; 2011. p. 245-52.

Thompson LU, Chen JM, Li T, et al: Dietary flaxseed alters tumor biological markers in postmenopausal breast cancer. *Clin Cancer Res* 2005;**11**:3828-3835.

Turnbull et al, Am J. Clin. Nutr., 55, 415-9, 1992.

Turnbull et al Am. J. Clin Nutr, 58, 507-10, 1993).

USDA Nutrient Database.

Vidueiros SM, Fernandez I, Bertero HD et al. Effect of quinoa (Chenopodium quinoa, W) on the intestinal mucosa of growing Wistar rats. FASEB J, Apr 2012; 26: 1033.4. 2012.

Watanabe I, Ibuki A, Yi-Chum C et al. Composition of quinoa protein fractions. Journal of the Japanese Society for Food Science and Technology (Nippon Shokuhin Kagaku Kogaku Kaishi)50. 11 (2003): 546-549. 2003.

Weisse K, Brandsch C, Zernsdorf B, Nembongwe GSN, Hofmann K, Eder K, Stangl GI: Lupin protein compared to casein lowers the LDL cholesterol:HDL cholesterol-ratio of hypercholesterolemic adults. Eur J Nutr 2010, 49:65-71.

www.drfuhrman.com/library/nuts-seeds.aspx.

www.foodallergy.org/alelrgens/tree-nut-allergy.

www.healthyeating.sfgate. com/types-beans-highest-amount-protein-6835.html, accessed 5/3/15.

www.livestrong.com/article/490658-chia-seeds-amino-acids/.

www.mycoprotein.org.

www.otago.ac.nz/humannutrition/research/nut.

www.thedailyspud.com/2011/01/6/potatoes-nutritionfacts/).

www.whfoods.com/gen-page.php?tname, accessed May 2, 2015.

www.whfoods.com/ genpage.php? Dbid=142 accessed April 28, 2015.

EPILOGUE

This book has highlighted the compelling evidence that a switch away from dietary intake of animal protein to plant protein can confer many health benefits. Not only may several common disease profiles be prevented or treated by the adoption of increasing vegetarian tendencies, this dietary switch makes ecological sense. An expanding world population cannot be sustained by reliance on animal sources of protein and calories which are an inefficient source of food energy with unhealthy consequences.

Evidence has been presented that traditional diets with excessive fat inclusions are not perceived to be damaging to health in people of certain ethnic origin e.g. the native Eskimo diet or diets rich in animal protein such as the Masai tribes in Africa. That said these traditional diets are changing as Western diets increase in popularity in all nations. The portability of Western diets threatens the health of many nations who continue to "beef up" (increase animal protein intake). Whatever the reason for the popularity or tolerance of these perceived unhealthy diets, it is clear that lifestyle factors play a role. The plant-protein eaters tend to have a healthier general lifestyle than the animal protein consumers in urban locations in Western society. Table 49.

- Healthier body weight
- Lower incidence of cardiovascular disease
- Lower rates of osteoporosis

- Specific advantages of monounsaturated fats
- Phytochemical benefits

- Low blood pressure
- Lower cancer rates
- Associated positive lifestyle

- Increased intake of dietary fiber
- Site specific cancer reduction: colon, breast and stomach

Table 49. Several health benefits of a plant protein (vegetarian) diet. Note vegetarians often tend to have healthy lifestyles with no smoking, low alcohol intake and greater exercise.

Individuals who move away from a standard Western diet can improve their health and help to prevent common killer diseases such as diabetes (Type 11), cancer, cardiovascular disease, obesity and osteoporosis. These health benefits of a more vegan existence can occur rapidly in a significant manner. Pivotal changes in this plant-based dietary shift are reduction in trans-fat intake, enriched sources of polyunsaturated fats, lower intake of damaging types of saturated fat, increased dietary fiber intake and nutrient or phytochemical intake from plants.

While the conclusion to "eat more plants" for health and wellbeing is clear, this dietary change still poses a major task for society. In Western society, the dominant sections of the food industry peddle processed food with high animal protein intake. Moves away from this situation will continue to be slow to occur and they have been underestimated in their potential benefits.

ABOUT THE AUTHOR

Dr. Stephen Holt is a best-selling author, medical practitioner in New York and Distinguished Professor of Medicine (Emeritus). He has been described as a visionary, a pioneer of Integrative Medicine and is world-renowned for his work on therapeutics with nutrition and dietary supplements. He is a frequent guest lecturer at medical and scientific conferences.

For many years, Dr. Holt has developed management pathways for several public health initiatives, with an emphasis on lifestyle changes and nutritional interventions. He believes that healthcare should be portable, widely available and free for children and the elderly. Dr. Holt has been described as the "doctor's doctor" because many of his patients are medical practitioners. Given the major pressure on Dr. Holt's time as an international lecturer etc., he restricts his patient care in New York to referrals only from other doctors.

He is an author of more than 20 books in the popular healthcare field and he has also contributed chapters and many articles to peer-reviewed medical textbooks and journals. As well as publishing several hundred scientific articles in leading medical journals, Dr. Holt has been cited thousands of times in the medical and lay press.

An honors graduate in medicine from Liverpool University Medical School, in England, UK, Dr. Holt holds sub-specialty qualifications in gastroenterology and internal medicine in the USA, Canada and Europe. He has practiced clinical nutrition medicine for four decades. Dr. Holt has held the rank of full professor of medicine and bioengineering adjunct for many years and he has received awards for medical teaching and research, in the United States, China, Indonesia, Great Britain, Malaysia, Thailand, Taiwan, South Korea and other countries, where he has served as a Visiting Professor. He now holds the highest academic rank as a Distinguished Professor of Medicine (Emeritus) at NYCPM.

OTHER BOOKS BY THE AUTHOR (Available for purchase at amazon.com and www.stephenholtmd.com).

Skinner HA, Holt S, The Alcohol Clinical Index, Addiction Research Foundation, Toronto, 1993

Holt S, Soya for Health, Mary Ann Liebert Publishers, Larchmont, NY 1996

Holt S, and Comac L, Miracle Herbs, Carol Publishing, Secaucus, NJ 1997

Holt S and Barilla J, The Power of Cartilage, Kensington Publishers, NY, NY 1998

Holt S, The Sexual Revolution, ProMotion Publishing, San Diego, California 1999

Holt S, The Natural Way to a Healthy Heart, M. Evans Inc., NY, NY 1999

(second printing 2002)

Holt S, The Soy Revolution, Dell Publishing, Random House, NY, NY, 1999 (third printing 2002)

Holt S, Natural Ways to Digestive Health, M. Evans Inc., NY, NY 2000 (second printing 2002)

Holt S and Bader D, Natures Benefit for Pets, Wellness Publishing, Newark, NJ 2001

Holt S, The Antiporosis Plan, Wellness Publishing, Newark, NJ 2002

Holt S, Combat Syndrome X, Y, and Z, Wellness Publishing, Newark, NJ 2002

Holt S, Wright J, Syndrome X Nutritional Factors, Wellness Publishing, Newark, NJ, 2003

Holt S, Enhancing Low Carb Diets, Wellness Publishing, Newark, NJ 2004

Holt S, Sleep Naturally, Wellness Publishing, Newark, NJ 2003

Holt S, Supreme Properties of Hoodia, Wellness Publishing, Newark, NJ 2005

Holt S, The HCG Diet Revolution, Authorhouse, Indiana, 2011 (www.authorhouse.com)

Holt S, The Antiaging Triad, Authorhouse, Indiana, 2011 (www.authorhouse.com)

Holt S, A Primer of Natural Therapeutics, Holt Institute of Medicine (2009) (www.stephenholtmd.com)

Holt S, Holt on: Sex The Natural Way, Authorhouse, Indiana, 2012 (www.authorhouse.com)

Holt S, The Definitive Guide to Colon Hydrotherapy, Holt Institute of Medicine (2013). Creative Space Publishing Platform

Holt S, Carroll C, Nwosu U, The Topical Pain Relief Revolution: Principles and Practice of Compounding Pharmacy, Holt Institute of Medicine, Creative Space Publishing Platform (2014)

Holt S, The Cannabis Revolution, Author House, Indiana, 2015

INDEX

alanine, 28, 30, 110, 140
    16, 19, 79, 108, 165, 180, 181, 186
albumin, 13, 37, 110, 139, 140, 143, 156
albuminoids, 13
algae, 166, 167
almonds, 23, 177, 178
alphalinolenic acid, 130, 169
amaranth, 23, 160, 187
    136
anti-bacterial compounds, 172
antifungal agents, 172
anti-helminthics, 172
antihypertensive, 85, 129
antinutritional, 155
antioxidant, 50, 56, 110, 124, 127, 163, 169, 170, 172, 175, 179, 183, 187, 188
antioxidants, 5, 12, 63, 81, 113, 117, 119, 127, 170, 175, 183, 190
antiviral medicines, 172
apoptosis, 61, 62, 125, 163
arabinans, 169
arginine, 27, 28, 31, 35, 42, 44, 73, 77, 98, 101, 102, 110, 111, 157, 16, 19, 31, 77, 79, 108, 164, 180, 181
Aspartic acid, 16, 165, 180, 182
asthma, 90, 144, 152, 153, 154
autism, 144
barbequed, 54, 59
barley, 37, 139, 141, 142, 143, 149
    137, 171
beans, 14, 21, 22, 23, 24, 29, 34, 52, 59, 130, 182, 183, 184, 185, 194, 51, 155, 182, 184
beta-carotenes, 161
biscuits, 59, 138
blood pressure, 12, 61, 64, 68, 82, 84, 85, 89, 96, 97, 99, 100, 121, 128, 129, 156, 167, 170, 175, 176, 177, 179, 190, 193, 196
Blueberries, 50
body building, 12
bovine, 43
Brazil nuts, 23, 176, 178, 194
breast, 42, 54, 56, 111, 117, 121, 125, 130, 131, 132, 134, 177, 179, 187, 194, 196
Broccoli, 30, 50
Brown Rice, 137
Brussel sprouts, 50, 51

buckwheat, 23, 160, 179, 180, 187
    136, 171, 179, 180
bulgar sorghum, 23
Bulgur, 30, 137
Cabbage, 50, 51
cakes, 138, 139
calcineurin, 110
Calcium, 26, 45, 73, 107, 145, 159, 160, 181
Calorie restriction, 59, 61, 63, 65
Calorie Restriction Mimetics, 61
cancer, 7, 8, 28, 42, 49, 52, 53, 54, 55, 56, 57, 58, 59, 68, 69, 70, 71, 72, 73, 75, 81, 86, 111, 117, 120, 121, 122, 124, 125, 127, 130, 131, 132, 133, 134, 136, 146, 163, 164, 166, 167, 172, 177, 179, 187, 194, 196
Candida albicans, 185
cannabidiol, 104, 105, 109, 111, 112, 115
Cannabis indica, 104
carbohydrate, 22, 38, 40, 67, 68, 72, 76, 78, 79, 130, 136, 137, 150, 170, 175, 184, 24, 160, 181
carcinogenic, 54, 56, 59
cardiovascular disease, 7, 28, 42, 44, 54, 55, 58, 59, 63, 64, 71, 130, 146, 187, 188, 192, 196
carotenoids, 56, 175
Carrots, 21, 50, 51
casein, 33, 43, 56, 77, 80, 83, 84, 97, 98, 110, 156, 158, 194
cashews, 23, 178
Cauliflower, 50, 51
celiac disease, 37, 80, 89, 139, 141, 142, 143, 146, 148
cereal, 37, 59, 81, 113, 120, 138, 139, 153, 154, 169, 170, 175, 179
cereals, 7, 23, 37, 49, 56, 139, 144, 149, 159, 170, 137
Cherries, 51
Chia, 2, 36, 155, 158, 159, 160
chicken, 55
chickpeas, 23, 59, 183
Chinese Chow Mein Noodles, 137
chiro-inositol, 179
chlorella, 166, 167, 168
cholesterol, 5, 7, 8, 10, 12, 24, 28, 50, 55, 57, 61, 64, 68, 78, 81, 82, 83, 84, 86, 89, 90, 91, 92, 93, 94, 98, 99, 101, 102, 113, 118, 121,

122, 124, 127, 128, 130, 132, 133, 134, 147, 156, 157, 163, 167, 173, 174, 176, 177, 179, 183, 184, 188, 194
Citrus fruits, 50, 51
coffeic acid, 175
colon cancer, 42, 179
complementary proteins, 13, 14, 22, 30, 49
copper, 129, 165, 175, 181
Couscous, 137
C-phycocyanin, 163
crackers, 139, 144
Cruciferous vegetables, 50
Cysteine, 16, 19, 180, 182, 186
Cystine, 79, 108, 164, 172
daidzein, 121, 123, 126, 128, 132, 184
Dark-green leafy vegetables, 50
dermatitis herpeteformis, 148
designer proteins, 155
DIAAS, 33, 34, 35, 77
diabetes mellitus, 5, 7, 8, 12, 42, 58, 59, 67, 111, 121, 130, 146, 174, 179, 180
Durum Wheat, 136, 138
Eastern Asians, 25
Edamame, 130, 155
eggs, 13, 15, 22, 24, 26, 49, 80
endometrium, 54, 131
ergogenic, 31, 40, 41, 48
esophagus, 54
essential amino acids, 7, 10, 13, 14, 16, 17, 18, 19, 20, 22, 23, 28, 30, 31, 33, 35, 37, 40, 49, 55, 85, 86, 88, 106, 108, 110, 112, 121, 149, 158, 160, 164, 173, 181, 184
Farm Bill of 2014, 105
fat, 5, 7, 8, 10, 24, 38, 42, 50, 55, 57, 58, 59, 62, 63, 64, 66, 67, 68, 81, 83, 84, 85, 91, 94, 109, 120, 122, 130, 134, 147, 150, 159, 170, 174, 176, 181, 182, 184, 196, 197
46, 70, 145, 148, 159, 160, 171
Fiber, 24, 46, 78, 79, 89, 148, 160, 171, 175, 191
fish, 13, 15, 22, 37, 41, 49, 55, 67, 85, 117, 120, 181
flatbreads, 139
flavonoids, 169, 175, 179
flax, 155, 177
for anti-aging, 60
functional food, 12, 115, 180
fungus, 173
Fusarium venenatum, 173

gallstones, 179
Garlic, 50
genistein, 121, 124, 125, 126, 127, 128, 132, 184
gliadin, 37, 139, 140, 142, 143, 146, 150
gliadins, 37, 139
globulin, 13, 37, 143, 156
Glutamic acid, 16, 165, 180, 182
glutamine, 37, 39, 139
glutelin, 13, 37
Glutelins, 37, 139
gluten, 37, 80, 86, 89, 99, 137, 138, 139, 140, 141, 142, 143, 144, 145, 146, 147, 148, 179
gluten enteropathy, 37, 80, 139, 141, 147, 148 142
gluten sensitivity, 141, 148
glycine, 27, 28, 37, 139, 140, 16, 19, 79, 108, 165, 180, 182, 186
grain, 49, 76, 81, 91, 138, 144, 154, 160, 170, 179
grains, 49
granola, 59, 113
Grapes, 51
Green tea, 51
Hard Red Spring Wheat, 136, 137
Hard White Wheat, 137, 138
hay fever, 144
Hb A1C, 68
heart disease, 49, 56, 57, 67, 68, 73, 81, 117, 120, 163, 175, 190
hederagenin, 172
hemp, 23, 104, 105, 106, 107, 108, 109, 110, 111, 112, 113, 114, 115, 116, 117, 118, 119, 155, 160, 177
Hempseed, 106, 107, 108, 109, 110, 116
heterocyclic amines, 54, 120
histidine, 18, 16, 17, 19, 79, 164, 180, 182
hives, 26, 144
hordeins, 37, 139
Hot peppers, 50
hyperoxaluria, 185
hypertension, 8, 12, 49, 96, 111, 128
hypertrophy,, 40, 89
Ice cream, 137
IGF-1, 28, 52, 53, 72
immune stimulators, 172
Inflammation, 65

202

insulin, 8, 12, 28, 31, 36, 53, 61, 62, 63, 64, 65, 73, 75, 78, 79, 80, 83, 88, 174, 192
iron, 12, 76, 81, 113, 125, 129, 130, 147, 161, 165, 166, 167, 177, 180, 181
107, 145, 159, 161, 181
isoleucine, 18, 76, 140, 170
        16, 17, 19, 79, 108, 164, 172, 180
Japanese Soba Noodles, 136
Japanese Somen Noodles, 137
kaempferol, 56, 169, 170, 183
Kale, 50, 51
Kamut, 136, 137
kidney, 42, 54, 97, 126, 128, 182
kukoamines, 175
lactose, 25, 86, 89
larynx, 54
lectins, 131, 155,147
Legume, 7, 22, 23, 30, 49, 51, 56, 66, 183
lentils, 23, 59, 180, 181, 182,29, 34, 155, 180, 181, 184
leucine, 18, 35, 69, 76, 77, 91, 110, 16, 17, 19, 79, 108, 164, 172, 180, 182
lima beans, 23
longevity, 52, 59, 60, 63, 65, 66, 69, 71, 72, 176
low glycemic index, 77, 93, 173, 179
lung, 54, 121, 125
Lupin, 155, 156, 157, 172, 190, 192, 194
lupins, 98
lysine, 18, 20, 23, 28, 31, 33, 43, 49, 51, 73, 76, 88, 98, 101, 102, 110, 157, 164, 170, 175, 182
16, 17, 19, 31, 79, 108, 164, 172, 180, 182
Magnesium, 107, 145, 159, 161, 171
maize, 23, 37, 43, 85, 139, 154
malnutrition, 19, 32, 59, 60, 63
manganese, 76, 159, 175, 181, 183, 184, 107, 145, 159, 161, 170
marijuana, 104, 105, 115, 117
meat, 7, 8, 13, 15, 22, 24, 41, 49, 54, 55, 57, 58, 59, 66, 67, 73, 74, 120, 130, 137, 140, 147, 148, 164, 173, 178, 181
Metabolic Syndrome X, 8, 24, 64, 65, 174
methionine, 18, 20, 28, 33, 43, 49, 51, 52, 76, 88, 93, 98, 102, 110, 118, 164, 181, 184, 16, 17, 19, 79, 108, 164, 172, 180, 182
microcystins, 166
migraine, 144, 151
milk, 15, 22, 24, 25, 26, 33, 43, 49, 56, 59, 80, 86, 113, 120, 121, 123, 172, 178

millet, 23, 137, 171, 190
molybdenum, 181
morels, 173
Mycoprotein, 155, 173, 13, 155
myricetin, 183
Niacin, 145, 159, 161
nitrates, 54
nitrites, 54
nuts, 22, 23, 30, 66, 80, 120, 175, 176, 177, 178, 179, 190, 192, 194
Oat Bran, 136
oats, 23, 34, 37, 139, 141, 142, 136
obesity, 5, 6, 8, 24, 49, 59, 65, 66, 92, 93, 94, 133, 146, 174, 175, 176, 183, 196
oligosaccharides, 155
omega 3 fatty acids, 130, 169, 170, 177
Onions, 50
ornithine, 30, 31
Oryza sativa, 77, 92
Orzyza glaberrima, 77
osteoporosis, 5, 7, 8, 15, 25, 42, 55, 58, 59, 68, 73, 100, 121, 126, 130, 196
ovaries, 54
pancreas, 54
Panthothenic Acid, 161
pasta, 23, 138
    137
pastries, 139, 144
PDCAAS, 26, 33, 34, 77, 110
pea, 11, 59, 76, 96, 97, 98, 99, 101, 102, 157, 193, 2, 34, 36, 76, 96, 97, 99, 100, 101
peanut allergy, 178
peanuts, 23, 26, 80, 178, 190, 34, 50
peas, 23, 29, 34, 59, 77, 96, 98, 101, 183
pecans, 23
phenylalanine, 18, 140, 16, 17, 19, 79, 108, 164, 172, 180, 181
phosphorus, 76, 165, 175, 180, 185
phytate, 155
phytates, 180
phytochemicals, 5, 12, 42, 50
phytolaccagenic acid, 172
pistachios, 51
Pisum sativum, 96, 101
plant, 5, 6, 7, 8, 9, 10, 11, 12, 14, 20, 22, 23, 28, 34, 35, 36, 37, 41, 42, 43, 49, 50, 51, 52, 53, 54, 55, 56, 57, 58, 59, 63, 65, 66, 67, 68, 77, 87, 98, 99, 100, 104, 112, 113, 114, 120, 121,

126, 127, 136, 139, 147, 148, 155, 156, 157, 158, 165, 169, 172,體 173, 181, 182, 183, 184, 185, 186, 188, 196, 197
polycyclic aromatic hydrocarbons, 54
poultry, 13, 22, 41, 49, 67, 120, 181
Prediabetes, 65
primates, 59, 60, 65
proanthocyanidins (PAC), 186
prolamin, 13, 37, 143
Prolamins, 37, 139
proline, 13, 37, 139, 140
prostate, 42, 54, 121, 124, 125, 128, 131, 177, 184
protease inhibitors, 155
protein, 5, 6, 7, 8, 9, 10, 11, 12, 13, 14, 15, 16, 17, 18, 19, 20, 22, 23, 24, 25, 26, 28, 29, 30, 31, 32, 33, 34, 35, 36, 37, 38, 39, 40, 41, 42, 43, 44, 45, 46, 47, 48, 49, 51, 52, 53, 54, 55, 56, 57, 58, 59, 61, 62, 63, 66, 67, 68, 69, 72, 73, 74, 75, 76, 77,78, 79, 80, 81, 82, 83, 84, 85, 86, 87, 88, 89, 90, 91, 92, 93, 94, 95, 96, 97, 98, 99, 100, 101, 102, 104, 105, 106, 108, 109, 110, 111, 113, 117, 118, 120, 121, 122, 123, 124, 125, 126, 127, 128, 129, 130, 131, 132, 133, 134, 135, 136, 137, 138, 139, 140, 141, 142, 143, 144, 145, 147, 148, 149, 150, 151, 152, 153, 154, 155, 156, 157, 158, 159, 160, 161, 163, 164, 165, 166, 167, 168, 170, 172, 173, 174, 175, 177, 180, 181, 182, 183, 184, 185, 186, 187, 188, 189, 191, 192, 193, 194, 196, 197

pumpkin, 23, 51, 55, 155, 189
purine, 185
quecertin, 169, 170, 183
quinoa, 23, 51, 160, 169, 170, 171, 172, 173, 187, 188, 189, 192, 194, 2, 29, 136, 155, 169, 170, 171, 172, 189, 192
Rapeseed, 108, 157
renal, 15, 25, 42, 63, 86, 87, 97, 99, 100, 121, 127, 181
rhamnogolacturonans, 169
Riboflavin, 107, 145, 159, 161
rice, 11, 14, 23, 25, 26, 33, 35, 36, 37, 43, 76, 77, 78, 79, 80, 81, 82, 83, 84, 85, 86, 87, 88, 89, 90, 91, 92, 93, 94, 99, 102, 139, 175, 182

Rice, 2, 6, 36, 76, 77, 78, 79, 80, 81, 84, 86, 87, 88, 89, 90, 91, 92, 93, 94, 108, 136, 137, 171, 181
rye, 23, 37, 102, 139, 141, 142, 143, 136, 171
sacro-ileitis, 144
salt, 8, 24, 59, 66, 139, 147, 169
saponins, 169, 172
sarcopenia, 12, 15, 53, 152
seafood, 80
secalins, 37, 139
seitan, 51, 140, 148, 29, 147, 148, 155
Semolina, 137
serajanic acid, 169
Serine, 17, 19, 79, 108, 165, 180, 182
sesame, 23, 80, 155
slow protein, 81, 97
smoking, 52, 196
Sorghum, 137
soy, 11, 22, 23, 25, 26, 33, 44, 59, 77, 80, 86, 88, 92, 95, 98, 99, 110, 113, 120, 121, 122, 123, 124, 125, 126, 127, 128, 129, 130, 131, 132, 133, 134, 148, 155, 157, 158, 172, 184, 186, 188
Soy milk, 29, 50, 123
Soy sauce, 137
soybeans, 33, 35, 36, 43, 80, 121, 122, 129, 130, 134, 148, 160, 182, 184, 29, 50, 182
spaghetti, 23
Spelt, 136
spirulina, 155, 160, 162, 163, 164, 165, 166, 167
stomach, 54, 79, 166, 196
strokes, 49
sugar, 37, 59, 61, 66, 77, 79, 89, 174
sunflower, 23, 155
Sweet potatoes, 50
tannins, 155
Teff, 136
tempeh, 120, 129, 148, 29, 148
thaumatin, 43
THC, 104, 105, 109, 114, 115, 119
The Genomic Research Initiative, 112
Thiamin, 161
threonine, 18, 20, 23, 33, 16, 17, 19, 79, 108, 164, 172, 180, 182
tofu, 113, 120, 123, 140, 147, 148, 29, 148
Tomatoes, 50, 51
Triticale, 137
truffles, 173

trypsin inhibitors, 129, 143, 180
tryptophan, 18, 20, 23, 28, 32, 33, 52, 55, 110, 184, 16, 17, 19, 79, 108, 164, 172, 180, 182
type II diabetes mellitus, 55, 65
tyramine, 185
tyrosine, 17, 27, 110, 125
    19, 79, 109, 164, 172, 180, 182, 186
valine, 18, 140, 17, 19, 79, 109, 164, 172, 180, 182
vegetable, 6, 8, 10, 11, 12, 37, 49, 50, 66, 67, 73, 80, 101, 120, 128, 154, 156
vegetables., 43, 52
Vitamin A, 159, 160
vitamin B12, 8, 161, 165
Vitamin B12, 161
Vitamin B6, 145, 161, 162
Vitamin C, 159, 160, 181
vitamin E, 176, 177
wheat, 23, 26, 29, 33, 34, 37, 80, 137, 138, 139, 140, 141, 142, 143, 144, 145, 146, 147, 148, 149, 150, 151, 153, 154, 155, 172, 187, 138
whey, 24, 25, 26, 33, 36, 76, 77, 78, 80, 81, 82, 84, 85, 86, 88, 89, 97, 186
White Corn, 137
Whole-Grain Wheat Flour, 136
Whole-Wheat Macaroni, 136
Wine, 51
Yellow Corn, 137
zein, 43
zinc, 129, 162, 165, 167, 181, 107, 145, 160, 161, 171

www.ingramcontent.com/pod-product-compliance
Lightning Source LLC
Chambersburg PA
CBHW060953230426
43665CB00015B/2181